LAUNCHING YOUR TEEN
INTO
ADULTHOOD

PARENTING THROUGH THE TRANSITION

Patricia Hoolihan

SEARCH
INSTITUTE
PRESS

Launching Your Teen into Adulthood:
Parenting through the Transition
Patricia Hoolihan

The following are registered trademarks
of Search Institute: Search Institute® and
Developmental Assets®.

Search Institute Press
Copyright © 2009 by Search Institute

At the time of publication, all facts and figures
cited herein are the most current available; all
telephone numbers, addresses, and Web site
URLs are accurate and active; all publications,
organizations, Web sites, and other resources
exist as described in this book; and all efforts
have been made to verify them. The author and
Search Institute make no warranty or guarantee concerning the information and materials
given out by organizations or content found at
Web sites that are cited herein, and we are not
responsible for any changes that occur after
this book's publication. If you find an error
or believe that a resource listed herein is not
as described, please contact Client Services at
Search Institute.

10 9 8 7 6 5 4 3 2 1

Printed on acid-free paper
in the United States of America.

Search Institute
615 First Avenue Northeast, Suite 125
Minneapolis, MN 55413
www.search-institute.org
612-376-8955 • 800-888-7828

ISBN-13: 978-1-57482-273-1

Credits
Editor: Susan Wootten
Book Design: Wendy Holdman
Production Supervisor:
  Mary Ellen Buscher

**Library of Congress
Cataloging-in-Publication Data**

Hoolihan, Patricia.
  Launching your teen into adulthood :
parenting through the transition / Patricia
Hoolihan.
     p.   cm.
  Includes bibliographical references and
index.
   ISBN-13: 978-1-57482-273-1 (pbk. : alk. paper)
   ISBN-10: 1-57482-273-X (pbk. : alk. paper)
   1. Parent and teenager. 2. Teenager—
Finance, Personal. I. Title.
HQ799.15.H66 2009
649'.125—dc22

                                     2009025514

About Search Institute Press
Search Institute Press is a division of Search
Institute, a nonprofit organization that offers
leadership, knowledge, and resources to pro-
mote positive youth development. Our mission
at Search Institute Press is to provide practical and hope-filled resources to help create a
world in which all young people thrive. Our
products are embedded in research, and the 40
Developmental Assets—qualities, experiences,
and relationships youth need to succeed—are a
central focus of our resources.

This book is dedicated with love to Chris, Caitlinrose, and Kelly James, my teachers and fellow travelers, and with gratitude to my parents, wise and loving souls that they are.

Contents

Preface   vii

Introduction   1

1 Dreams (and What It Takes to Get There)   5

2 Senior Year: The Emotional Roller Coaster   17

3 Exploring Work, Service, and Other Paths   33

4 Looking for the Right College   47

5 Money, Money, Money: Learning to
   Handle It Wisely   75

6 Navigating the Financial Aid Maze   83

7 Preparing Your Teen for Independent Living   101

8 Living at Home after Graduation   115

9 Independent Living (and All That Comes with It)   121

10 Pack, Unload, and Leave   129

11 This Is It! The Parenting Shift   137

12 Supporting Your Teen's Problem-Solving Skills   145

13 Your Teen and You: The Emerging
   Adult-to-Adult Relationship   157

14 Honoring the Parental Passage   163

Resources for Parents and Teens

   • A High School Time Line for Parents and Teens   175
   • The College Application Package   179
   • Key Dates for the High School Senior Year
     Calendar   180

Bibliography   181

Acknowledgments   187

Index   189

Preface

When our daughter left for college, I was shocked by the way her physical absence resonated within me. The walls of her empty bedroom echoed, and the echoes reverberated inside my skin. Gone—the baby, the toddler, the sturdy young girl, the special and especially energetic teenager. And vanished into thin air—my role as a day-to-day parent, sometimes hands-on and at other times hands-off. A quiet emptiness mixed with pride, satisfaction, and even relief welled up inside. This was surprising to me, given the moments in her senior year when our teen was so difficult to live with. At times, a part of me (*and* her) had been ready to immediately launch her on her own.

Friends felt similarly bereft. We helped each other along, but found little written about this important emotional transition for parents. Everywhere I went that year, I overheard parents sharing stories about teens who were heading toward the door to begin the next chapter of their lives. A muted sense of loss formed the backdrop of these conversations. Shouldn't we be happy our children were moving on? Isn't this how it was supposed to be?

But loss is a funny thing—it is seldom singular. One loss triggers thoughts of another, past and future. As one parent remarked, "It's so hard to be left behind." Some parents may wonder how this transition will alter their lives and change their primary focus. A psychologist admitted that she cried a little every day in the months after her youngest left for college. In her practice, she says, "I see this specific loss all the time—it's a big issue."

Not every parent views the transition with only sadness, of course. There is pride, too, and satisfaction in having prepared a teen well for the next step. Whether you greet the changes that accompany your teen's passage through high school and beyond with joy, sorrow, or something that's more difficult to name, it *is* a time to reflect upon your accomplishments as a parent and the inevitable transitions in your relationship with your child. This book offers you reassurance and resources to meet the challenges and transitions you'll face as you adjust your parenting strategies and provide the support your teen needs along the passage to adulthood.

—Patricia Hoolihan
July 2009

Introduction

In high school, teens stretch themselves in many directions—academically, socially, physically, and emotionally—and they need parents whose flexibility allows them to grow into competent, independent young adults during this transitional period.

One father wondered how he could parent his son in a respectful, "hands-off" way when his son decided to live at home after high school to work and attend a nearby community college. The father wanted to prevent the worries he had for his son's future from infecting their good relationship. Importantly, he recognized that his concerns arose in part from his own experiences, and he understood that it would be counterproductive to project them onto his son. Still, it's not easy to change the way you parent, even when insights like this one dawn. As you prepare to launch your teen, you'll find support in these pages for shifting your parenting style toward a solid advisory role that can serve you well into the future.

This book focuses on the crucial years of preparation—all of high school, really—and situations parents face in the first months and years after launching teens. *Launching Your Teen into Adulthood* explores the factors that make up that successful launch: what it takes to prepare young people for life after high school, help them define and move confidently toward their goals, and cope with challenges along the way. Anecdotes from parents who have already made the passage are included here to shed light on your own experience. Each chapter ends with a "to-do" list of practical items that remind you to communicate clearly and guide with a sure touch.

The following topics are addressed:

- **Chapter 1, Dreams (and What It Takes to Get There),** offers helpful questions, tools, and resources for encouraging teens to begin to think about future careers, college, technical training, and other post–high school experiences.
- **Chapter 2, Senior Year: The Emotional Roller Coaster,** focuses on the final year of high school and its demands on parents and students alike.
- **Chapter 3, Exploring Work, Service, and Other Paths,** summarizes a variety of post–high school alternatives to college.
- **Chapter 4, Looking for the Right College,** lists helpful resources for conducting a college search and walks parents through practical ways to assist teens with this task.
- **Chapter 5, Money, Money, Money: Learning to Handle It Wisely,** discusses the all-important money management topics that teens need to understand to be money-wise.
- **Chapter 6, Navigating the Financial Aid Maze,** outlines important steps for parents and teens when applying for financial aid, grants, and scholarships.
- **Chapter 7, Preparing Your Teen for Independent Living,** contains advice on preparing to move out, important parent/teen conversations, and parents' shifting roles.

- **Chapter 8, Living at Home after Graduation,** provides a thoughtful approach to parenting teens when they continue to live at home after graduation.
- **Chapter 9, Independent Living (and All That Comes with It),** covers issues of health care, roommate and personal relationships, alcohol and substance use, different lifestyles, and more.
- **Chapter 10, Pack, Unload, and Leave,** provides helpful ideas to prepare for and finesse the big moving day.
- **Chapter 11, This Is It! The Parenting Shift,** explores ways parents can stay connected to teens and find the balance that supports a teen's independence and problem-solving.
- **Chapter 12, Supporting Your Teen's Problem-Solving Skills,** offers tips for supporting teens as they figure out their own solutions to problems and determining when parental assistance is necessary.
- **Chapter 13, Your Teen and You: The Emerging Adult-to-Adult Relationship,** takes a creative approach to bonding with teens as they emerge into adulthood, offering snapshots of various approaches and reminders to parents that there is fun to be had in the years ahead.
- **Chapter 14, Honoring the Parental Passage,** suggests ways parents can acknowledge their own parenting accomplishments and hopes for the future.
- **Resources for Parents and Teens** provides additional tips, including "A High School Time Line for Parents and Teens," "The College Application Package," and "Key Dates for the High School Senior Year Calendar."

- The **Bibliography** offers a wealth of suggested reading on topics related to values clarification, assessing the job market, college admissions, essay writing, and more.

If you were planning to sail along an unfamiliar waterway, you'd first study maps, identify navigational markers, and devise strategies for coping with the unexpected. In the same way, you can use this book and its resources to guide you through the new territory ahead. Everything changes as our children enter their late teens, and exponentially so. They can drive, they can vote, and they take up so much more physical space! No longer are they merely passengers in your boat; rather, they become co-navigators in some stage of launching their own craft alongside you. The beauty of the trip, then, is in acknowledging the passage as you travel together, and keeping an intentional eye on the destinations ahead: theirs *and* yours. It is a remarkable journey.

CHAPTER 1

Dreams (and What It Takes to Get There)

If one advances confidently in the direction of his dreams, and endeavors to live the life which he has imagined, he will meet with a success unexpected in common hours.

HENRY DAVID THOREAU

The high school years and the first years beyond are times of transition—passages from one place, condition, or action to another. Ultimately, all teens must answer the question "What do you want to be when you grow up?" and work through the steps that will lead them to their destinations. While some of our own peers settled early on their life's work and pursued it single-mindedly, many, many others entertained ideas that fell into the "needs more exploring" category. The people in this group experimented with several careers and pursued multiple interests. Our children are likely to do the same.

As adults, we can relate to teens who aren't sure which direction to take—there are so many different directions they *can* take. This awareness of a teen's dreams and goals is an important part of parenting. Acknowledging your teen's ideas for the future is one part of helping prepare her or him to make choices and set goals that she or he can weave into school, work, and relationship choices.

How do we help our children make the kind of informed choices and plans that will ensure meaningful futures? How do we help them reach for their dreams while factoring in the realities of financial and situational limitations? One school counselor maintains that it is so important for parents simply to be with their kids during this transition. Go for coffee with your teen, travel to schools or potential job sites together, and listen as he figures out what he wants and needs to do next. Favorite meals or family movie nights can be counterpoints to frequent parental nudges about meeting deadlines. Teens need to sense that the home is a place of relaxation and comfort, a place where they can "chill." Often, so much is going on in their lives that they don't even realize the full impact of all that intensity.

Exploring Passions and Supporting Dreams

Adrienne Diercks is founder of the Minneapolis-based Project SUCCESS, a nonprofit organization that supports middle school and high school students as they transition to school, work, and beyond. Diercks says her organization "encourages kids not only to think about their dreams, but also to take action toward making those dreams come true by identifying and defining practical goal-oriented steps." She says parents need to acknowledge that "kids are dying to be heard." Over and over, the number-one suggestion offered by Diercks and youth leaders, school counselors, and education professionals is that parents listen—really *listen*—to their kids and spend time *being with* them, a key part of empowering them to make good choices.

When a teen tells Diercks that her goal is to attend Harvard (or the local university or school of culinary arts), or find an apprenticeship or enlist in the military, she first asks, "What do you know about this school (or program)? And what is it that makes you want to go there [or try that]? Let's do some research together to find out more about this option." If a teen says to his parents, "I think I want to be a firefighter," Diercks suggests that parents ask similar questions. "What do you know about this type of job? What about it appeals to you? Would you like to talk with someone who has been a firefighter for 20 years?" She makes a point of connecting teens in her program to mentors who can continue the conversation in a useful way, even if the outcome propels a teen in another direction.

Diercks says teens often feel inundated by questioners who ask them what they want to do when they grow up. They experience a good deal of social and cultural pressure as a result. Sometimes it's helpful to acknowledge a teen's need for a break from that pressure. And at times, it's just wise to ask gentler, less pressure-filled questions, such as "How are you doing today?" or "Senior year can be so stressful—how is it going for you?" or "What good things happened to you today?"

Since the future is never very far from a teen's mind (or yours!), simply spending time together can encourage the kind of goal clarification and processing that teens need to do to make good decisions. This soul-searching passage has several components, and having discussions with adult "guides" is one of the most important. Research is also key, as is making good use of available resources, of which there are many.

Naming Goals and Defining Steps

What are your child's dreams? What are his gifts? What are her interests? How does he want to provide a living for himself in the world? What does she want to contribute to making the world a better place for others? The late teen years are a wonderful time for individual exploration, but they are also a time for focus, even if a teen's focus is slow to become clear.

Ask your child at key points—the start of the school year and the beginning of a new activity—what her goals are. Setting goals is so important, as is outlining the steps needed to achieve them. You can model effective goal-setting by mentioning some goals you've achieved and by continuing to demonstrate your own learning. Be sure to talk about progress toward your goals and the steps they will require. Share new things you've learned along the way.

During our daughter's high school years, her athletic coaches were helpful in articulating the process of visualizing dreams and planning the steps that would make them a reality. It's what good coaches and mentors do and they do it all the time, often with real skill. For this reason, nurture your teen's connections to coaches, youth leaders, theater directors, teachers, club sponsors, caring relatives and neighbors, and other special adults in her life.

A coach or other activity leader may provide your teen with a goal sheet to fill out and post in a visible place. There is something very powerful about looking regularly at written goals to help you think about the daily steps involved in reaching them and to feel that they are worth achieving. Many life lessons are learned through goal-setting, which can deepen and enrich a teen's journey throughout these years of transition.

A friend relayed the story of a businessman who had built his company from scratch. He wrote down his goals—both big and small—on pieces of paper he kept tucked inside his pocket. This businessman could physically touch his goals, often and daily. Those scraps of paper were touchstones, especially important at times when he felt disappointed or tired.

Borrowing the idea, this mother encouraged her son to write his goals on self-stick notes. Since anything left in his pockets was likely to disappear, she encouraged him to post the notes on his wall, around his picture frames, on the bathroom mirror, or in another highly visible spot. Her son is now out in the working world. On a recent visit home he spotted some of those old goals still posted around his childhood room—goals for tennis matches, term papers, and college applications. Seeing the old notes brought so much back—for the young man and his mother. They realized how many goals he had met as he pointed them out, one by one. Not all of them, but many.

As a parent, you do have the wisdom of hard-earned experience. Work with your teen to help him map the steps involved in reaching a goal and consider the realities of finances and personal skills, as well as other related factors. Help your teen put finances in perspective by discussing how spending and making money are part of his plans and goals. The unpredictable economy has an impact, of course, on our children and their choices. Grappling with economic realities is a must.

One of our ongoing jobs is to show enthusiasm for our children's vocational exploration. Encourage your teen to make the most of available contacts and opportunities. Be honest about how much and in what ways you can help, and communicate any limitations. Armed with clear information and support, teens can make competent choices and set worthwhile goals.

Connecting Goals with Resources: Mentors, Personality Inventories, and More

One of the great things about interested friends, neighbors, aunts, and uncles is that inevitably people will ask of an older high school student, "What are your plans for next year?" or they query a college student, "What subject are you majoring in? What classes are you taking? What are you excited about or interested in studying?" Even if a teen can't specifically answer such questions, they make a good exercise for thought and discussion. And it's useful for teens to get input from and be engaged by other adults.

Teens benefit greatly from meeting with adult mentors and conducting informational interviews with professionals working in their fields of interest. A police officer neighbor or nurse anesthetist relative can be a great source of information for a teen hungry to learn more about these careers. And how about the resident actor in your neighborhood? She would be happy to meet with your teen, especially if one of you lets her know ahead of time that your teen is interested, and your teen follows up with a phone call or e-mail reminder. Members of faith communities and local civic groups are also frequently willing to provide career mentoring, which can be a distinct asset to teens.

Taking a Self-Assessment

Encourage your child to connect with available resources that allow him to identify his strengths, interests, and motivations. An excellent self-assessment tool is an interest inventory (on paper or online), which helps teens zero in on their strengths. The Self-Directed Search, an interest inventory created by psychologist John Holland, and others, such as the Myers-Briggs Type Indicator personality assessment and the Kuder Career Planning system, can give your teen a clear idea of his strengths, talents, and interests. Interest inventories are frequently available through school counseling offices. If not, many are also available free online or for a small fee. When your teen takes a self-assessment, set aside time afterward to discuss her results. For more information about interest and career assessments, see Chapter 4, Looking for the Right College, page 47.

Exploring Text Resources

With your teen, you'll want to check out these useful resources for investigating options after high school (available at your local library):

- *Occupational Outlook Handbook* by the U.S. Bureau of Labor Statistics
- *Occupational Outlook Quarterly* (online at www.bls. gov/opub/ooq/ooqhome.htm)
- *Fiske Guide to Colleges* by Edward B. Fiske
- *The College Board Book of Majors* by the College Board

Sometimes parents and teens are tempted to view existing possibilities through a narrow lens, so browsing through these books cracks wide open the world of future possibilities.

The first handbook, revised and updated every two years, explores hundreds of jobs of all kinds. The *Occupational Outlook Handbook* describes the training and education necessary for most jobs and covers the expected salary, job conditions, and tasks that a person actually performs on the job. This book reveals job possibilities that currently exist in the workplace, as well as providing students and parents with information about future trends. The related *Occupational Outlook Quarterly* is updated four times per year and provides a current overview of the labor market.

The *Fiske Guide to Colleges* offers a wealth of detail about most four-year college and university programs in the United States and is updated annually. And you and your teen will find that the *Book of Majors* underscores the truth that there are many ways to use one's talents and abilities. This book provides teens with an expansive view of available career choices and study options. It, too, is updated on an annual basis. See the Bibliography, page 181, for many other resources that address career and college themes.

Trying Out Experiential Programs

Other excellent resources are experiential in nature, including programs you may discover locally like the previously mentioned Project SUCCESS. These programs use discussion, role-play activities, and relevant work experiences to help kids figure out who they are and what they want to do with their lives. Isn't that ideally what we as parents want to help our teens do? Urban communities throughout the United States feature similar school and work support programs for teens, and can be identified by contacting your school counselor or local community and technical college.

Taking Dreams for a "Test Drive"

As your teen's high school graduation approaches, talking about college and other post–high school experiences is also the time to continue conversations about dreams and goals, passions and plans. Some kids have a clear idea of the field of study that interests them; others are open to exploring a variety of possibilities. Sometimes it's not until much later in college, technical school, or on the job that a certain professor, class, or mentor opens up a new world of interest to a young adult. This intellectual exploration can be one of the most exciting parts of post–high school study. It is in pursuing interests and making choices that a teen's focus emerges, whether through work, study, travel, service, or a combination of these.

If college is a teen's chosen path, the first year or two will be all about academic exploration. It's the second half that is set up for students to begin narrowing their choices and choosing majors. If your child opts for a different path—work, service, travel—he will also be very much involved in the exploration process. Keep asking about his experiences. It is good for teens to articulate the events that are shaping their dreams and goals. Keep the focus on the big picture. Remind your teen not to let today's girlfriend, party, or fresh disappointment keep him from moving steadily toward the dream/goal he is working on. At the same time, encourage your teen to continue looking for reasons to enjoy each day.

Since life is generally a series of goals to be imagined, worked toward, achieved, sometimes deferred, and occasionally shelved, parents can model this understanding and think aloud with teens about the steps involved to plan for their reality. Part of what we do for our kids is show that we continue to set goals, work steadily toward them, and enjoy the process along the way. Becoming a whole person involves circuitous routes; ultimately this transformation is connected to our self-awareness and self-knowledge. A certain degree of these qualities is required to create viable dreams—and visualize working routes toward them.

Deferred Dreams

Sometimes dreams must be put on hold or re-envisioned. Things happen: a family crisis, a death or illness in the family, a teen pregnancy. Or the program to which a teen has attached his dreams turns him down. How do you help your teen through disappointment or the need to temporarily defer a dream? It can be helpful to know that others who have had to defer their dreams were able eventually to pursue them. Nevertheless, disappointment is not easy to navigate.

Mia, a college student in her 30s, spoke of marrying early and becoming pregnant at age 16. She had two more babies at 19 and 25. With her third child balanced on her hip, she explained that she had never given up the idea of going to college. Mia had made an earlier attempt after the birth of her second child, but could handle the simultaneous demands of parenting and school for only two semesters before a pending divorce took her down. However, she picked herself up, healed, and kept her goal in mind.

Now in a stable, supportive relationship, Mia has worked out a child-care arrangement with her mother and sister and is back in school, where she is a straight-A student. She spoke of writing papers while her baby napped or early in the morning before the children awoke. Part of what motivates her is the prospect of being a positive role model for her children. Mia will be the first in her family to get a college education.

Working through Disappointment

Sometimes a teen must absorb his disappointment and open his mind to new possibilities. It helps when parents offer their compassion and support, rather than criticism and judgment.

John was turned down by a New York theater program that he had set his heart on. His favorite high school teacher helped him see that his second choice could be an excellent fit. He entered a program closer to home—without the prestige of the first choice but with a good reputation. For a period of time, John felt sad and bitter.

Halfway through his freshman year, he began to appreciate his professors and the close access to them that a smaller school provided. When his younger brother ended up having surgery, John was glad to be close by. At numerous times it occurred to John that he had ended up in a very good place, and it was perhaps even better in many ways than the program that had turned him down.

When Family Illness Intervenes

Shelley's mother was diagnosed with cancer in the spring of Shelley's senior year of high school. Although she was seriously considering attending a college halfway across the country, she knew in her heart of hearts that she couldn't bear to be so far away during her mother's crucial treatment period. She opted to attend a community college close to home and deferred her first choice for a year. The time Shelley spent with her mother and younger sister during the following year was time she did not regret. As her mother recovered, the first school began to re-emerge as a possibility. In her sophomore year, Shelley was able to transfer—the school had held a place for her.

Dreams as Leaders

Dreams are better thought of as leaders than as dictators. There is no such thing as only one way to fulfill a dream. And dreams are wonderfully malleable. They can adapt and grow, adapt and grow again. Sometimes the contours of a dream shift due to life's unpredictable circumstances, but you can teach your teen that the core of her dream can be kept alive and pursued. If your child struggles with disappointment, help him find others who were able to hold on to their dream or adapt their dream and pursue it over time in spite of initial obstacles. Obstacles can be great teachers, and they can strengthen sense of purpose.

HELPING TEENS IDENTIFY GOALS

➤ Listen, spend time with, and encourage your teen in her vocational search.

➤ Ask your teen about his dreams and plans for the future. Suggest that he write down one or two important goals. Help him list the steps for reaching the goal, and the available resources to support that goal.

➤ Look for opportunities—in the car, while doing chores together, or at the dinner table—to ask questions about your teen's classes and teachers.

➤ Ask her about the people she admires in the neighborhood or faith community, or at her job or volunteer work.

➤ Visit the library with your teen to browse the College Board's *Book of Majors,* Edward Fiske's *Fiske Guide to Colleges*, and the U.S. Bureau of Labor Statistics' *Occupational Outlook Handbook.* See the Bibliography, page 181, for other helpful resources.

➤ Encourage your teen to ponder goals and write them down. Post the goals where he or she can see them every day.

➤ Be available to help line up and use available resources: Look around your family, neighborhood, faith community, or workplace for mentors, information, and programs your teen can tap. Don't wait for an organized program to come along in order to help your teen set up an informal mentoring network.

➤ When disappointment strikes, as it inevitably will, help your teen revise or set new goals.

CHAPTER 2

Senior Year:
The Emotional Roller Coaster

One day I'd want to pull my hair out (or hers!) if she draped her purse, backpack, books, and coat once more over the kitchen table, and then . . . I'd find myself watching her dance in the final dance performance with tears rolling down my cheeks. She was so graceful, so talented—she had worked so hard for this moment. I was so deeply proud.

FATHER OF A HIGH SCHOOL SENIOR

Her senior year was filled with intense emotion. On any given day you could find us fighting, crying (from joy or frustration), slamming doors, or heading outside for fresh air and a walk to cool down. Either we were being eaten alive by hormones . . . or we had begun the most difficult process yet—letting go. I think it was both.

JULIANN HEATH, "THE LETTING GO"

You find yourself preparing for your son's hockey awards banquet and it hits you—after years of driving him to practice and centering your social life around his games, the absolute *last* hockey event of his high school career is at hand. And when the awareness hits, you happen to be opening a pack of napkins for the banquet table. Suddenly, you need one of those napkins for the tears that come. Unbidden. Unstoppable. Your emotional response is likely to be the same even if, just the day before, he responded to a simple question from you with "Why do *you* want to know?" and you thought to yourself, "I can't *wait* for college."

Not all parents feel overwhelmed by a sense of loss at the prospect of their teen's departure, but many parents do comment on the moment they become suddenly and powerfully aware that their child will soon leave home. End-of-season events are rituals that give meaning to the "good-bye" process. They provide opportunities for photos and video clips that will stand as mementos of the good times. School and extracurricular ceremonies focus on the special qualities of what was so great and what is now drawing to a close. Entire senior casts have been known to burst into tears after the final curtain call of the annual musical. It all tugs at the heartstrings, for parents and teens alike.

Families sometimes speak of how difficult this transition feels. One family, midway through their child's senior year, described the stresses their daughter felt from a heavy class load and the extra work involved in applying to schools. She was unsure of her top college choice even in December, and worried about being accepted. Her father had been sick, and the family, coping with high stress levels at home, felt a kind of early grief already setting in. The father sensed a huge shift—his only child, to whom he was very close, was on her way out of the nest.

Caring for Yourself and Finding Support

Part of the intensity of a teen's senior year is that so many events are overlaid with a heightened awareness of endings and new beginnings. As excited as they are about what lies ahead, parents and teens feel a tinge of loss in their celebrations; the familiar halls, activities, and friendships will all be shifting in the months ahead. Where do parents turn in the midst of this shift? To each other.

Actively supporting one another through this phase is enormously helpful for fathers and mothers alike. Take comfort in knowing that other parents understand the strange, bittersweet mixture of emotions. The sadness you may feel about your impending loss (of focus, of day-to-day parental love in action, of your own parenting identity) is one that you don't want overshadowing your children's momentum. Even though teens may harbor their own mixed feelings, many are *absolutely* looking forward to being out on their own. And that's a good thing. It's the transition for which you have been training and preparing them all these years.

Suddenly, those years seem fleeting. And popular slogans make it sound easy: Cherish the good times; love them and let them go. Yet it is challenging for parents to sift through ambivalent emotions and prevent powerful feelings from interfering with kids' needs. That's why having someone else to talk to—another parent, a supportive group of friends— can make all the difference.

Asking for help in maintaining your personal health is appropriate and sometimes necessary, whether it's from a best friend, through a parent group, in individual counseling, or through some other form of self-care. One woman whose mother died early in her son's senior year was motivated by the combination of events to call a counselor for extra support: "I wouldn't have made it through without her help, without knowing I could see her regularly and process the feelings that . . . roiled around inside me." A teen's senior year is often so laden with emotional ups and downs that when parents experience another major life event, it can strain their coping abilities.

Part of your parenting job during the maelstrom of senior year is to take time to do whatever it is that keeps you energized: exercising daily, spending time with friends, reading a good book. It is a year that demands a lot of a teen and, by extension, a lot from you. So, as your energy gets used up, be conscious of ways to rejuvenate and re-energize yourself. Staying centered and steady as a parent, especially during the tension-filled senior year, makes a positive difference. You can be most available to your teen if you are calm and take care of your own needs.

Feeling Grief and Loss

Janet, a parent in her 40s, called her best friend the day after her daughter's senior track banquet. "I was a mess last night. I just realized how much I am going to miss her. I have been so involved in her activities." Janet and her daughter had been close and enjoyed similar interests and hobbies. She had attended many of her daughter's events and often volunteered. It was fun, and Janet had developed a social life around these events, enjoying the company of other parents.

Janet also ran her own business. She had figured out a way to do so with flexible hours. Still, she felt an impending sense of loss, especially after the banquet. That day she just needed to talk about everything—and not to her daughter, but to an adult who understood. Her friend, who had recently been through her own child's senior year, could empathize. "You just have to go through it, there's no way around it. And hang on, honey, there are still months of these final events left for you. Be kind to yourself—what you're feeling is like a mild, and sometimes not so mild, form of long-term grieving."

When the sadness welled up, her friend's words were a

comforting reminder to be kind to herself, to write about her feelings in a journal or talk about them with friends. The advice helped Janet remember that part of the parenting voyage involves feeling occasional pangs of loss and being aware of the love between mother and daughter—a gift that continued to be a precious part of her life.

Excitement about the Future

For Heather, any sadness about her son's growing up and moving on was mitigated by the fact that in his last two years of high school, he had blossomed and grown out of his shy reserve, eventually developing a strong group of friends who appreciated his interests. Watching this transformation, Heather felt happiness and relief that overshadowed any twinges of loss. Those came later, when her son left for college.

Not one to call much, and only an infrequent e-mailer, Heather's son communicated less than she would have preferred, but she knew that he would be in touch when he needed to be. While she really missed being able to see him and hear about his life, Heather had, above all, enjoyed watching him emerge as a young adult during this transitional time.

Saying Good-Bye So Soon

Although a teen's actual departure can be gut-wrenching, parents may notice that settling into daily life without a son or daughter may prove not nearly as difficult as the anticipation of it.

Jen's daughter's entire senior year was intense. It reminded her of the months leading up to her daughter's earlier coming-of-age bat mitzvah ceremony at 13, when Jen had recognized that she was preparing her child to eventually leave home. That senior year, Jen cherished the evenings her daughter and friends gathered in the kitchen to bake cookies. But as fun and enjoyable as the final rituals of senior year and graduation parties were, Jen often found herself tearing up in anticipation of her daughter's departure.

A particularly difficult day was the occasion of her daughter's absence from the family Passover meal. Her daughter had taken a high school trip to the city where she would be attending college. Although Jen expected that she would eventually celebrate holidays without her daughter, she was not prepared for the sadness she felt. After taking a long walk, which always helped her feel better, she returned to find a cheerful phone message from her daughter: "Mom, I'm having such a great time—I love this city! The sun is out; we are exploring all over; and when I move here, I am never leaving!" Jen's daughter was already dipping into her next life and talking about never leaving it. Jen could see that it was time to begin discerning next steps for herself and simply had to laugh about how happy her daughter seemed.

Staying Calm through the Push/Pull of Separation

In her essay "The Letting Go," Juliann Heath writes, "It seems to happen overnight. They go to bed one evening adoring you, and they wake up the next day ignoring you. . . . I felt the teenage years were necessary to help me release my daughter into the [world]. Had she always remained a pre-adolescent, I would never, ever, have been able to let her go."

If you don't have a sense of humor, cohabiting with your teen is going to be a rough ride. As one single parent of teens says, "If you can't laugh, you may as well check yourself into the psych ward!" Amen. Especially during the months that lead up to applications and deadlines, a teen's resistance to suggestion and tendency to procrastinate bump right up against a parent's need to guide wise choices. Anxiety beats like a drum, and unpleasant rhythms too easily emerge— crabbiness, resentment, rising tempers. Humor is key.

During this time, any tricks you may have to calm anxiety—yours and your teen's—should be pulled out of the hat each day. One mother said she became a faithful practitioner of yoga. Its focus on breathing and stretching always helped to calm her. A father of teens said that continuing to play music with his band helped him focus on what really mattered. Another father struggled to get along with his son, who argued with him about writing his college essays. This father happened upon a lucky moment of understanding when he asked gently whether his son felt fearful or anxious about the process of preparing to move on. His son spoke openly about the anxiety he was feeling and his fear that everyone except himself would get into college.

A Difficult Senior Year

Senior year was tough on Lisa and Jim, but it was tough on their son, too. He was often defiant, felt he clearly knew more than either of his parents, and argued that he should have the freedom of someone who was already living on his own.

Lisa and Jim found themselves doing the hard work of constantly setting boundaries as their son pushed up against each one. Their teen's late nights were followed by the loss of car privileges. He faced similar consequences for stumbling in one night smelling of beer. At the same time, the couple worked hard to stay in touch with all that their son was going through in terms of trying out new things and making difficult choices. Parenting on the cusp of this "letting go" process can be quite emotionally draining.

Lisa had to remind her son repeatedly—up to the last minute—of looming deadlines until he finally filled out whatever current form was due. Jim and Lisa survived—some days they were worried and crabby; on better days, they were filled with a sense of humor and the knowledge that they had a right to expect certain courtesies from their son. He was a tough senior, as some of them are. But on graduation night, they also understood how much they would miss his wonderful energy, his easygoing nature, and his ability to lovingly tease them. This—in spite of joking with their friends about all the things they wouldn't miss. Ironically, their son called them often for support during his freshman year.

A Bittersweet Change of Schools

At times a teen must change schools in the midst of the high school years. The new choice that you and your teen make may represent a better fit for your child or be the result of a move or a change in the family, but regardless, it will come with certain challenges. Parents usually try to carry on and convert a sometimes-difficult decision into a positive one (as you would want your child to do, too). But if you feel a loss of community once the change is made, you can bet your teen also experiences it.

Pam's son changed schools in his junior year for a combination of academic, athletic, and peer group reasons. It dawned on her several months into her son's senior year that she was grieving the loss of an experience that many around her were having. Instead of participating in events in which she and her son were surrounded by friends they had known for years, the two of them were observing final senior milestones with kids her son was just getting to know and parents who had long since formed bonds that

Pam did not share. She was aware of the difference between her experience and that of her close friends.

The realization snuck up slowly, though, not coming fully to light until Pam had a conversation with a cousin whose job had required frequent moves. "It's a very different senior year if it's spent in a new environment, instead of in one where years of relationships have been built—it's lonely." Pam had been trying to figure out why it had all felt so hard, and her cousin's acknowledgment of this particular loss finally helped her understand the process she was going through.

Pam made a point of asking her son if he, too, missed the old school. He responded, "Not the school—but I do miss my coach and I miss my old gang. I see them on the weekends, but it's not like being with them every day." He was able to immediately name who and what he missed. This uprooting added an extra layer of grief to the normal separation process. The key for Pam was to talk to someone who really listened and learn to understand her feelings, a healthy way to move toward letting go.

Coming to Terms with Regrets and Imperfection

The biggest mistake I made is the one that most of us make while doing this. I did not live in the moment enough. . . . I wish I had not been in such a hurry to get on to the next thing: dinner, bath, book, bed. I wish I had treasured the doing a little more and the getting it done a little less.

ANNA QUINDLEN, *LOUD AND CLEAR*

Endings and beginnings invite a new perspective, a moment for reflection. In a writing exercise her senior year, our daughter described what she regretted not doing during her high school years—experiences and people she hadn't opened herself up to. Although there was sadness to her realization, it was also helpful for her to write it down. Writing gave her a particular awareness that she could carry into the next chapter of her life.

Certainly as parents we have some regrets—about trips not taken together, rituals that could have been created years ago, influences to which we wish our teens had not been exposed. This sense of inadequacy hounds us all. But as parents, we need to realize that we *have* done a good job, and while it may not have been perfect, it was likely good enough. And given the passion, commitment, and 24/7, 18-year cycle of day-to-day parenting, who doesn't experience peaks and valleys? All that active parenting translates to thousands of days and hundreds of thousands of hours. No parent can possibly be "on" all the time, functioning always at one's best. Whatever our vulnerabilities are, they are not lost on our children, and the next child in our lives can benefit from this awareness.

Coming to terms with regret is part of the coming-to-the-end-of-an-era process. We didn't enjoy our kids enough, we weren't tough enough, we weren't gentle enough, and so on. Ultimately, this struggle is about coming to terms with being imperfect. This is harder for some than for others. We sometimes forget that being human is more important than being perfect. As I examined my own regrets, it helped to realize that my relationship with my teen was not over. Some of what I felt I had missed could be incorporated into our new future.

Our daughter couldn't wait to live on her own. Yet in the years since she's been away, leaving home has given her a deeper appreciation of her father and me as parents, and we have shared some wonderful times together. The physical separation has allowed us to see how much we enjoy each other and how many interests we have in common. I worked hard during her senior year not to take her sometimes-distant attitude personally and to continue loving her in spite of her occasional disdain. It wasn't difficult to admire her many fine qualities, but what *was* hard was being on the receiving end of temperamental moods and the times when she thought her parents knew so little.

Mark Twain is said to have remarked that "when I was a boy of 14, my father was so ignorant I could hardly stand to have the old man around. But when I got to be 21, I was astonished at how much the old man had learned in seven years." It's true. And there will definitely be days ahead when we need our friends to remind us that we are still smart, capable, and fun to be around.

Dress Rehearsal for Departure

Maureen, a mother of three, didn't experience her oldest child's departure as a huge shock because he simply wasn't around that much during his senior year. Instead, he spent a good deal of time with friends, and when he was home, often shut himself in his room to play the guitar and compose music. Maureen adjusted to less of his physical presence around the family. In a way, her son's actual leave-taking was gradual, because he was rehearsing it in the many months beforehand. Although it was sometimes difficult and sad, Maureen eased into the new reality. And with two other children's needs to focus on, there was plenty to do.

Final Senior Events

If senior year is a roller coaster ride, the last two months are the final minutes of the ride. This is the steepest climb of all—final exams and deadlines, making *the* choice, attending end-of-the-year events, and locating baby photos to display in the yearbook or at a reception. Then there's the most windblown and exhilarating speed of the final descent—the flurry of open houses, celebrations, and the graduation ceremony itself. For most parents, those senior-year moments have special poignance: listening to teens perform in one last concert, watching them play in one last sporting event, hearing their names announced and watching them cross the stage to receive their diploma.

Almost every other evening seems filled with some "last" event. In the midst of it all, your son or daughter may still be vacillating about a work plan or a school choice, or you may find yourselves fitting in an unexpected, last-minute visit to a vocational-technical school or college campus. By May 1, though, your teen will probably have made up his or her mind about what comes next. Of course, there will still be deadlines and details to take care of, and seniors will still need to study for final exams and check that their transcripts are complete.

Sandwiched among all those final obligations, you may decide as a family to hold a special dinner or open house to celebrate your teen's successful completion of school. Be sure to include your son or daughter in the planning, and take pleasure in the choices he or she makes. While it's nerve-racking to juggle the activities of senior year with party planning and ensuring your home makes a good impression, try to keep a balanced perspective that allows your family life and work responsibilities to have their place, too. Stay organized with to-do lists that you and your teen review periodically, and consider calling a family meeting to enlist everyone's help.

May and June are a time when many paths of effort converge. The senior roller coaster ride ensures lots of fun and plenty of wind in the face because the pace is nonstop. Off and on, tears will come. Not only are you about to send your own child into the wider world, but there's an awareness that this particular community of teens and parents you and your teen have been a part of is about to scatter. You may be able to keep up with some, but it will require extra effort. The built-in focus you shared—on school and activities—is widening, and you can't help but feel it, even as you cherish its special qualities. One father commented wistfully, "You know that all-night graduation party? I swear it's for parents to grieve what's ending. Enjoy *all* those special events."

Diplomas, Tassels, and Handshakes

Graduation day finally arrives:

Abby came home with her graduation cap and gown; I made her put it on days before commencement. I needed time to digest this pill. She also informed me that she and a couple of other students from her American Sign Language class had been asked to sign the national anthem at the commencement. My daughter confidently walked her 5'10" slender, blonde, pierced nose, engaged body up onto the stage as if it were just another day in a crowded school. The anthem started to play, and her hands began to gracefully dance as she communicated the words. . . . It was truly one of the most beautiful things I had ever seen. I am one who is always moved by our national anthem, and to see it expressed through my daughter's hands was . . . beyond words. My eyes filled with tears that marched down my cheeks in the same fashion that the seniors had streamed into the auditorium. There was no holding back the pride; I did a swan dive right into the Kleenex box.

JULIANN HEATH, "THE LETTING GO"

Whether you celebrate graduation with a private family dinner or a gathering for neighbors and friends, this is the time to appreciate who your child has been and who he or she is becoming. It's powerful stuff. More than anything, I urge parents to treasure these days. It's not important whether your child was an academic star or just an okay student, a team player or a solo artist. What is important is that you celebrate your teen's friendships, accomplishments, and interests, whatever they may be. These are the last days of an era for your family—an era that you and your teen have navigated together, even if imperfectly—and it is the beginning of an entirely new period in your teen's life.

So hang on to your hat. Enjoy the ride. Sleep when you can! Try to maintain a bit of serenity. Senior year is a stressful time because there is simply so much to do. But it's also a time for gratitude and for acknowledging this huge rite of passage for your teen—and you.

KEEPING AN EVEN KEEL

- Make time to attend and cherish special events.

- Allow yourself regrets, but follow them with appreciation for all you have done and shared with your teen.

- Tuck away quietly in your mind at least one thing that drives you crazy about your teen—hold it close in the tough moments of letting go.

- Let your teen know what makes you proud of him or her.

- Talk regularly to your good friends or a trusted counselor about the mixed emotions coursing through you.

➤ Remind yourself often that the intensity you feel is part of the "senior in high school" deal—you're not crazy. The year *is* manageable, and you are definitely not alone.

➤ Expect May and June to be incredibly busy. Put every event on a calendar.

➤ Start digging up those special family photos for memory books, photo boards, and so on. Don't wait until the night before the yearbook deadline or party day. Remember, you only need a handful.

CHAPTER 3

Exploring Work, Service, and Other Paths

It is always challenging—and often rewarding—to take the path less traveled. Good options exist for teens who aren't yet ready for or can't immediately afford college, or for whom college simply does not feel like the right choice. Learning can take many forms. If your teen is drawn to work, community service, or travel, there are ways for him to continue to learn and build life skills.

Vocational-technical schools and community colleges give young people incredible, focused training for jobs that guarantee work and a living wage. A writing student of mine trained as one of the first female pipefitters in my area. She knew that, at any point, she could find a job and make good money. In a volatile economy, there is much to be said for learning and mastering a practical, hands-on trade.

A full-time job can be an invaluable learning experience for teens—one that teaches accountability, personal responsibility, and bankable skills. The right job for the right teen can be a productive match during the first year (or longer) out of high school.

"It's hard to find a gap-year student who will tell you it didn't help make them a better and more motivated person. Sometimes, the path to growing up is the one less traveled—but that's for you and your teen to decide," says writer Jeanne Muchnick in the e-newsletter *Parenting Teens Online* (www.parentingteensonline.com).

Community Service Programs
That Make a Difference

For teens who have a strong calling to do community service work, are not academically motivated, or need more time to mature, there are several excellent options that provide structure and focus. National programs centered on full-time service include the federally funded Job Corps; AmeriCorps State and National; AmeriCorps Volunteers in Service to America (VISTA); and AmeriCorps National Civilian Community Corps (NCCC). Many faith-based organizations also direct their own community service programs for older teens.

Job Corps

Job Corps was founded in 1964 as a valuable community work program for young people with limited financial resources. Participants must have income below a certain level; other than that, anyone between 16 and 24 who is a U.S. citizen is eligible. Job Corps centers can be found all over the United States, and their primary purpose is to train young men and women for the work world, often in a skilled trade. The program will also help participants complete a General Education Development diploma (GED) if they lack a high school diploma. Job training can take anywhere from eight months to two years, and participants receive a monthly allowance. Centers are set up like colleges, with on-campus dormitories. The program also helps place graduating students in the workforce.

AmeriCorps

AmeriCorps encompasses three different programs: Ameri-Corps State and National, AmeriCorps VISTA, and Ameri-

Corps NCCC. All are service-oriented programs, providing teens with an opportunity to serve the community where help is needed through a variety of ways—from tutoring children to building homes. All three programs require that a participant be a U.S. citizen, but the age requirements and focus differ slightly. Most plans prefer or require a yearlong commitment.

AmeriCorps State and National accepts applicants 17 and older and employs them all over the country wherever a need exists. Many participants in this program have played a part in rebuilding Louisiana in the aftermath of Hurricane Katrina. Some learn hands-on home-building skills, others work in health-related jobs, and still others tutor children. Participants are paid a modest monthly allowance, receive health coverage and child care (if applicable), and can qualify for an AmeriCorps Education Award that may be used to pay for qualified vocational school, college, or graduate school expenses or to repay student loans. In addition, program participants experience the intangible but real benefits of improving the lives of others.

AmeriCorps VISTA requires that adult participants be a minimum of 18 years old. Teens often work alongside older people; the program draws a fair number of retired persons. This program prefers participants who have some college education or work experience, and looks for people who are flexible, organized, and self-motivated. Fluency in another language, especially Spanish, is an asset for this program. The service focus is helping in poverty-stricken areas.

AmeriCorps NCCC is a 10-month, team-based residential program designed for young people between the ages of 18 and 24. Education level is not as important to this program as a person's energy level. Teens in this program are trained in public safety and CPR techniques and may find themselves clearing trails and streams, tutoring children, rehabbing low-income housing, or responding to natural disasters. Participants live in groups of 10 to 12 in one of five AmeriCorps communities in California, Colorado, Iowa, Maryland, or Mississippi. As with the other programs, AmeriCorps NCCC addresses a wide range of community needs and offers teens opportunities to learn and practice skills that last a lifetime. For more information and to apply for all the AmeriCorps programs, see www.americorps.gov.

➤ ────────────────────────────────────

Lost and Found: Setting College Aside for Service Work

John's son, Alex, was one of those kids who felt a bit lost in college. By nature, Alex was easygoing and social, and he had had a good time at school—perhaps too good a time. However, his learning disability had made college academically challenging. After a couple of semesters at two different community colleges, Alex felt frustrated with his academic progress and started to talk about traveling. A friend invited him to hang out on a Florida dive boat for the winter, which John was pretty sure would involve copious amounts of drinking and possibly drug use as well.

Alex was ready to be out from under his parents' roof. He wanted to leave home and prove himself. But he was the type of person who had trouble motivating himself and did better with some structure to his days. John seized upon Alex's interest in travel but suggested travel with a focus on service. John and Alex did some research on AmeriCorps, and Alex and his parents sat down to talk about it. The idea sounded better than just hanging out on a boat, even to Alex. After researching his options, Alex applied and was accepted by the AmeriCorps NCCC program. He headed first to one of the program's training campuses in Maryland.

AmeriCorps NCCC begins with an intensive three-week training program. Strict in its approach to discipline and physical fitness, the program has participants start their days at 5:00 a.m. with exercise and a run. During the day, classes include lifesaving training, interpersonal skill building, and group discussions of ethical issues that sometimes arise in community living. Each project that AmeriCorps NCCC adopts provides a slightly different living experience for participants, but all groups live together in a manner similar to college dormitory life. Participants share rooms and common space. On some assignments in particularly impoverished neighborhoods, they might sleep on cots in rather bare-bones conditions.

Once training is complete, participants are assigned a work project—the first of several they are given during their service year. Work experiences are called "spikes" and last roughly two months. During his AmeriCorps NCCC year, Alex was sent to five different spikes, each distinctive in nature. Every experience is organized for a team, often composed of three males, three females, and a supervisor. The groups cook, plan meals, and grocery shop together, sharing the food expenses as well. Financial and community living topics are part of the learning experience. Participants also learn a great deal about who they are and what it means to be of service in a world with many needs.

Alex's experiences included working for Habitat for Humanity to help rebuild hurricane-damaged homes along the Mississippi Gulf Coast. He worked with at-risk kids in New York City and assisted with ground cleanup in Yonkers, New York. In New Orleans, Alex worked on home repair in the aftermath of Hurricane Katrina, sometimes leading volunteer groups coming in from all over the country. He also worked in Galveston, Texas, preparing and delivering meals in the wake of Hurricane Ike. Finally, in Camden, New Jersey, Alex tutored schoolkids, focusing on environmental themes while living in a poverty-stricken neighborhood. He spent the year surrounded by other young adults, all of them environmentally conscious and service oriented.

Alex's friends say he came home a changed person. John and Alex both say that Alex's AmeriCorps year gave him self-confidence and more clarity about who he was and what he wanted to do with his life, leaving behind his somewhat fearful "me" focus to adopt an outward focus on the "other."

Traveling to Learn

One post–high school option that focuses on experiential learning and travel is the Wyoming-based National Outdoor Leadership School (NOLS) program, which organizes wilderness experiences both inside and outside the United States. A semester with NOLS can be applied toward college credit; the costs are comparable to state school tuition. NOLS offers a wide range of outdoor experiential learning trips including backpacking in the Southwest; mountaineering in the Rockies; and skiing, sailing, or sea kayaking as far away as New Zealand. The NOLS curriculum emphasizes wilderness skills, leadership, and environmental ethics, and teaches orienteering, emergency first aid, self-reliance, and practical outdoor survival strategies. For teens with physical energy who love the outdoors and are interested in experiential education, the NOLS program can build confidence, self-esteem, and deeper self-awareness. For more information, visit www.nols.edu.

The Independent Traveler

Julie and John's daughter, Jenny, decided early in her senior year of high school that she wanted to spend part of the following year in a theater internship and part of the year in service work overseas. She did much of the research and legwork on her own. Her parents initially hesitated until Jenny described her well-conceived ideas and they realized they could be productive growth experiences for her.

They ultimately gave her their approval contingent on Jenny's acceptance to college and receipt of a one-year enrollment deferment. Jenny agreed, realizing that if she was doing service work abroad the next spring, it would be difficult to apply to college at the same time. Jenny organized a fall internship with a local theater company, helping out in the office, assisting with a fund-raiser, and trying her hand at assistant directing. She arranged to spend her second semester working in an orphanage in India.

As challenging as it can be for even the most laid-back parents to think of their teen leaving home and perhaps heading to a distant country, there is a time for each parent to step back. When a teen is given permission to move toward a vision that she sees clearly and articulates carefully, the next logical step for a parent is to let go and respect what that young adult can do.

Jenny's parents faced two difficult moments during their daughter's time overseas. The first was seeing her off and waiting to hear of her safe arrival a day and a half later. The trip was long and a lot could have gone awry, especially during the long stretches when cell phone service was not available. Once they heard Jenny had arrived safely, mother and father could breathe a sigh of relief.

The second challenge came when their daughter called to say that she was very sick. Hearing the news, they felt helpless being so far away. Jenny had to help herself manage through that difficult period and ask for help from others in her sponsoring organization. She recovered, but not before her parents experienced three days of heart-wrenching phone calls in the process. When another person working with Jenny became ill and had to be hospitalized, Jenny helped care for her. She sat with the woman in the hospital, checking on her daily. Upon recovering, the woman sent Jenny's parents a thankful e-mail telling them how brave and compassionate their daughter had been and how she had helped the woman so much through a difficult time. Said Julie's parents, "We still have that e-mail posted on the wall. It's the best progress report you could imagine."

Their daughter returned strongly enriched by both semesters spent out in the world. She entered college the next fall; although she expected to find herself a year behind in terms of making connections and friends, the transition was a smooth one. If anything, college may have seemed too tame after negotiating her way around a foreign country, dealing with poverty in its many forms, and coping with a wide variety of trains, planes, and bus stations. But Jenny soon chose an area of study that was challenging and compelling, and she was quickly absorbed by it.

For parents, there is a lesson here. It is natural for parental fear or concern to be part of your response to your teen's decision not to follow the norm and stray from your expectations. The key is to remind yourself of your teen's many strengths and not let your misgivings interfere with your child's path. Julie's parents experienced huge rewards: they discovered how self-sufficient, brave, and caring their daughter was. They watched her grow as she challenged herself. They had always loved Jenny, but now found her to be a human being who was even more interesting and impressive than they had ever imagined. The payoff for letting her go was to see clearly how they had raised a daughter who was independent, bright, capable, and compassionate.

Thinking outside the Box

Research and knowledge of a teen's interests has a payoff for both parents and teens. By using all the contacts at your disposal, through school career and counseling offices and post-secondary admission offices, you can identify focused ideas and leads that might well lead you to discover good matches for your child's skills, abilities, and interests. Your encouragement can provide the motivation your teen needs to take the next step, forming a vision for his future.

One mother spent her break time visiting her son's school counseling center to research high school programs for her son, hoping she could help him find his way despite the family's limited financial resources. She discovered a summer program between high school years that was offered by a local technical school. Her son decided to enroll.

At first he considered an auto mechanics course, but later switched to graphic design to capitalize on his interest in art. With his mother's support, he participated for two summers in the program and did well enough that, as a high school senior, he was awarded a full two-year scholarship to the trade school. He was able to live at home and graduate with an associate's degree in graphic design, which qualified him for both employment and further schooling.

Choosing a Skilled Trade

Gentle reminders of what it takes to reach a goal that matters to your child can motivate him and help him understand how important today's steps and choices are in shaping his future.

Sandy's second child was a born mechanic—always fixing things, always interested in cars, always happy to hang around his dad's auto repair shop. When he graduated from high school, he went right to work for his father. He also enrolled in an auto mechanics program at a nearby technical college, taking classes two nights a week. He needed a lot of encouragement to keep going, because he learned that already he could earn what he considered a good salary as a rookie mechanic, and often felt he knew as much as his teachers. It was hard for him to make school a priority. But his parents reminded him that if he wanted to open his own shop one day, he would need to have his auto mechanic's certification and the practical skills that business and communications classes could give him.

Choosing Public Service

As parents, we can keep our eyes and ears open for the kinds of opportunities that match our children's interests. Sometimes, using informal contacts and networks, parents can help teens find and arrange hands-on career explorations that help teens make informed decisions about both what they want to do with their lives and, importantly, what they *don't* want to do. Unpaid on-the-job training and internships are excellent ways for teens to check out a career or field of interest.

Cody thought he wanted to become a police officer. His parents had heard about a community-based program called Police Explorers, which gives high school kids the opportunity to meet local police officers and learn about criminal law, police investigations, and other aspects of police work. Cody's school counselor helped him complete the necessary paperwork to enroll in the program and get permission to participate on some school days. The program proved to be a great way for Cody to explore his interest in police work. He discovered, though, that the part of police work that really appealed to him—helping people in need—was sometimes secondary to other concerns that didn't really fit his vision.

Instead, as a high school senior, Cody decided to pursue firefighting. Several of his friends' fathers were firefighters, and they filled him in on the details of the job. Cody learned that to be a firefighter, he needed to be 18, be able to read, and be in good physical condition. And he also learned that if he eventually wanted to advance in the firefighting profession, and be able to work in ambulances as well as on the fire truck, he would need a two-year associate's degree to become a licensed paramedic. This became his goal.

Enlisting in the Military

Nate applied to three colleges the fall of his senior year in high school. But he was also drawn to the U.S. Army and ultimately chose to enlist. He says:

> When I did service work through my church and traveled to several different countries, I really came to see the freedoms we have here in the United States. I have a strong bond with my grandfather, who served in World War II, and after considering several career and school options, I felt I was most drawn to carrying on the work my grandfather began. I want to devote the next few years of my life to defending the freedoms of our country. And when my service is up, I will also be able to get an affordable college degree.

Nate's father had chosen a different path for himself, getting an education deferment during the Vietnam War. It was hard to accept Nate's choice, but he was also moved by the bond between his son and his father, and could see how Nate's admiration for his grandfather influenced his decision.

Yes, I feel the fear of every parent who has a child in the military. I don't want Nate to be sent to a war zone, but I can see that he will get a good education in the army and learn discipline, and he is so interested in this option that I can't stand in the way. I try not to focus on my worries and just support him. It is clear this is what he wants to do.

When your child chooses to join the armed forces, one of your jobs as a parent is to find a way to let go of the decision, having faith in the wisdom of your teen's chosen path. Life and death situations loom larger in this field than in others, but the rewards of a military career can also be great. As a parent, you are not alone in your concerns for your teen's safety; remember that you are part of a larger group of parents and families who have supported loved ones in service to our country for generations.

When Your Teen Is a Family Trailblazer

If your child is the first family member to go on for more training after high school, it's helpful to understand that this can be a lonely road. It requires leaving behind a family pattern and a familiar way of life. Your encouragement and support of your teen's choice can outweigh the pressure he may feel in making such a choice.

William, a senior in high school, came to the United States from Nicaragua when he was 6 years old. Although his mother had always told her children that she expected them to go to college, he was the first to actually attend.

I try not to focus on that too much because I feel too much pressure to succeed. Instead, I focus on getting my nursing degree and being able to earn money and have my own apartment and make enough to be able to help my mother out.

He sifted through several ideas before settling on a plan. At one point, William considered enlisting in the military because of the academic and financial benefits it would later provide. But he decided he didn't want to postpone his degree. He also thought about working in the construction trade because he knew others who already did. But William also had learned to look at the big picture and decided that he valued earning a degree and getting a job in a field that he could work in for the rest of his life, without being limited by the physical demands of the work.

Nursing appealed to William because it combined physical activity, service to others, and steady work. He enrolled in a nearby community college and was admitted to a special program that paid for his first two years of college while he is living at home and studying full time. He plans to complete his general education requirements and then apply to a four-year registered nursing program to complete his degree. What helps William stay focused on his goal is how much he wants the kind of job that will meet his goals and give him economic security. And support from his parents (and other caring adults) has proven most helpful to him.

When you support your teen's desire to pursue post–high school options—whether it's work, public service, trade school, an apprenticeship or internship, junior college, or some other path, you express your faith in his ability to make decisions for himself. There will be challenges along the way, as there are with any life choice, but your confidence in his decision sends a strong message that will strengthen the effectiveness of your parent-child bond.

EXPLORING WORK, SERVICE, AND OTHER PATHS

➤ If academia is not your teen's strong suit, or if he feels the need for a break from the pressure of a school setting, start talking about other possibilities.

➤ With your teen, research alternative options. Sometimes it helps to put ideas in front of your teen.

➤ Information about AmeriCorps, NOLS, and other programs is available online. Start with www.americorps.gov and www.nols.edu.

➤ Check out local and regional programs. Your teen's school counselor or college and career center staff have more information on various post–high school options.

➤ Have the courage to consider unconventional alternatives for your teen. Then encourage your teen to recognize many opportunities off the straight-to-college path.

➤ If your teen is an "outside-the-box" kid looking for an "outside-the-box" experience, help her research jobs, internships, and travel opportunities. Use all of your contacts, including people from work, the neighborhood, your faith community, and organizations to which you belong.

➤ Encourage your teen to interview a person who has successfully taken an alternative route after high school. This can be an excellent opportunity for your child to get a different perspective worth considering.

CHAPTER 4

Looking for the Right College

My condolences to you for being immersed in a senior year.

SPOKEN HUMOROUSLY BY AN EXPERIENCED
MOTHER OF FIVE, WITH ONE SENIOR TO GO

S enior year has a very special quality to it. For most parents and teens, it is jam-packed, busy, and intense. It is also an exciting time, ripe with potential and meaning. When your teen chooses to pursue college studies after high school, the rush of application deadlines and school choices dovetails with end-of-the-year senior high school and extracurricular events to create an emotionally charged atmosphere. Your teen is moving toward decision-making time, and that carries pressure affecting everyone in the household. All the parental herding needed in these final months of figuring out what comes next is equally tough on kids and their parents. Watch, help, and support your teen as he sifts through his choices, keeping in mind how huge the looming transition is. Even as teens push against the boundaries of home and parents, they are questioning their choices and their future.

The Research and Application Process

One of the best things that comes out of the college search is the sense of self and optimism about the future students

can gain if they search thoughtfully. You can help them by
asking questions.

COLLEGES THAT CHANGE LIVES WEB SITE (www.ctcl.org)

The importance of the research phase cannot be emphasized enough. The number of resources and choices is abundant and often overwhelming. Experts suggest beginning the research phase as early as possible. Juniors and even freshmen and sophomores can benefit from gathering information early on about where they might want to go. Since certain colleges and many major areas of study require specific coursework, it is a definite advantage to begin looking and planning ahead.

Research happens in several key ways: through online searches; reading books that are purchased or borrowed from libraries; visiting the high school guidance office or college and career center; connecting with visiting college and technical school representatives; and talking to current or former students of schools in which your teen is interested.

What to do after high school is a huge decision, so clarity often comes only by senior year. The research phase, no matter when it is begun, becomes critical by the end of the junior year and into the senior year of high school. And of course kids at this age are still in the process of growing and developing—their interests are continually being shaped. No one really knows at 16 what she wants to be when she grows up, but hopefully a person has some clear inkling of her interests and abilities and the direction she wants to head.

Online Research

Most teens are quite comfortable with online searches. This becomes a real asset as they research the next step of their lives: future occupations, colleges, alternative training programs, apprenticeships, and more. Most likely our children will be more skilled at this kind of research than we parents are.

Naviance.com, an online career and academic guidance program for teens and parents, is used by many public and private schools. It is currently available to students and their families free of charge when their schools order a school subscription. Naviance.com features a search engine that provides interest-inventory surveys and matches a teen's skills and interests to available programs and schools. Your student can search for information about tuition rates, school locales, academic programs, and more. This guidance tool is offered through high school college and career centers, and students may also have home access through their personal computers.

Unigo.com, an online college resource created in 2008 by a recent college graduate, features audio, visual, and written information from current students about college campuses around the United States. While most other information systems describing universities and colleges are written by marketing professionals and administrators, this search program stands out for its close up and honest look at campus life from an insider's point of view. Jonathan Dee, a writer for the *New York Times Magazine,* says, "[Unigo.com] changes the game from an economic standpoint, too: it costs a lot of money to travel far away from home to check out schools, and Unigo.com offers an unfiltered, detailed, often somewhat eccentric view of campuses all over the county. A 45-second video in which an unseen student pans around the courtyard at Sarah Lawrence . . . is so evocative that it makes the one-page *U. S. News and World Report* summary—or the descriptions in Sarah Lawrence's own admissions catalog, for that matter—read like junk mail" ("The Tell-All Campus Tour," September 18, 2008).

Guidebooks

Throughout our daughter's junior and senior years, the *Fiske Guide to Colleges* was like a bible around the house. It's a hefty paperback—8½ by 11 inches and several inches thick—and as bulky as a metropolitan phone book. But it seemed to hold the potential of the world within its covers. An endless supply of self-stick page tabs proved a good accompaniment. A fairly comprehensive report on colleges across the country, this guidebook lists available majors, admissions test score and grade point average requirements, and tuition and room and board costs as well. It contains vital information for most colleges and universities in every state, and sometimes offers brief personal quotes from current students. The *Fiske Guide* also provides details such as total enrollment, numbers of males and females, percentage of returning freshmen, relevant phone numbers, and admissions Web sites.

A teen can peruse this book and mark the programs and places that interested him the most. He might try a color system, using yellow to mark first-choice affordable schools, purple to mark first-choice expensive schools, orange to mark second-choice schools, and so on. The number of sticky tabs might become overwhelming, but this process or one like it can help lead to making a clear decision.

Another excellent guide is Loren Pope's *Colleges That Change Lives*. This book examines some of the smaller, lesser-known colleges that have reputations for accepting and working wonders with kids who may not be academic all-stars. The book's guiding principle is the belief that there is a solid college match possible for every kind of student. Contrary to the myth that is prevalent in many high schools, a useful, productive, and solid education can be found at many, many colleges around the country (including those close to home), not just at exclusive Ivy League schools. Divided into geographic areas (the northeast, south, midwest, southwest, and northwest), this book is filled with interviews of professors and students. It offers a personal feel for each campus while also imparting clear information on available degree programs and other opportunities.

Pope writes, "While no one really knows, the estimates are that 12 to 20 percent of the population has some kind of learning problem." *Colleges That Change Lives* is a great guide for students who are academically challenged in any number of ways—from dyslexia to test anxiety to information-processing issues to a host of other challenges. The colleges Pope writes about focus not only on students' difficulties but also on their strengths and ability to succeed. The opening chapter title conveys the mission clearly: "Today's 'learning disabled' will be tomorrow's gifted and the SAT's obsolescence."

If your student is an actor, artist, writer, musician, or dancer and is interested in further pursuing these creative skills, then an excellent source of information would be *Creative Colleges* by Elaina Loveland. The author not only explores colleges and what they offer, but also provides helpful examples of how to audition and what to put together in a portfolio. Admission to art-based schools is often dependent on a young person's portfolio of creative work. How to best display a teen's ability for a potential school is a significant part of the process. This book is filled with tangible hands-on advice and hints.

These are certainly not the only guidebooks available. Many other excellent guidebooks can help with general information or a specific focus. For instance, in addition to books for those interested in the arts, there are guides written for teens interested in nursing, psychology, and the military, as well as guides that address the needs and concerns of African American and Hispanic teens. If you have a specific focus, these books can save a lot of time. See the Bibliography beginning on page 181 for a more extensive list of resources.

Parents as Guides and Advisers

Colleges That Change Lives and the companion Web site (www.ctcl.org) remind parents that "you can guide [teens] by asking useful questions, such as what they like about the college, what they think they will major in, and what career path they may pursue. The answers to these questions may change as your student learns more about his or her values, goals, and priorities, so check in often to see what they're thinking."

As guides for our own daughter, one of the things we could do was point out people she could talk to who were familiar with certain schools and parts of the country that she considered possibilities. As parental guides, we can gently steer our children toward helpful resources, or, if we are lucky enough to have a "self-motivator," we can cheer him or her on. Some parents will need to be more hands-on than others, but by now you probably know exactly which kind of kid you have.

You may have friends working in professions that genuinely interest your teen. Helping her set up an informational interview with one of these contacts can be an excellent way to support her interests. "My daughter spent an entire work day with my friend, a hospital chaplain. She went on rounds with her, visiting patients and their family members. It gave her a real feel for a profession she is seriously considering," one mother told me.

Underlying this research phase are internal questions that can be challenging for teens to navigate. Grappling with this process represents a giant step toward adulthood. It requires self-knowledge, making difficult choices, and a great deal of planning. Although it sounds obvious, sometimes as parents we get so consumed by deadlines that we forget to take time to ask questions and listen to what our teens are really thinking.

Keeping Deadlines Front and Center

A major cause of family feuds in the final year of high school can be missed deadlines. Avoiding this situation may be as simple as scheduling a regular check-in with your teen on goals and timetables regarding program choices. Don't underestimate the importance of a checklist and highly visible calendar! Invite your teen to help you set up a detailed calendar and keep it handy. These deadlines are the mile markers along the journey. Of course, the challenge is discerning when to prod and when to step back. The posted schedule of deadlines is a parental aid that helps take the heat off your role. After all, it's not just *your* schedule; it belongs to your teen and the world he is in the process of entering. A helpful suggestion is to use bold print or color coding on the schedule—anything that keeps it from sliding into the background.

For most parents, senior year is so much about keeping your teen on task with applications, tests, and homework. One mom said, "I hope this isn't how he remembers me, and I hope this isn't how I remember parenting him. Or we will both be toast! There's so much reminding and hounding; I'm tired of hearing myself." A couple of months later, she was excited about her son's acceptance to one of the colleges on his list. By that point, all the work of encouraging him seemed well worth it.

During this time, there are several goals to keep your

eyes on. The main one is to help your child find her way in the world. Since you know her so well (remember to focus on who she is and not who you want her to be), your input or guidance can be instrumental. Also, many teens just plain need reminding (everything from picking up dirty socks to meeting that college application deadline). The calendar posted on the kitchen wall, the checklist that is not buried under other paperwork—both are essential tools for student and parent alike. See "A High School Time Line for Parents and Teens" and "Key Dates for the High School Senior Year," pages 175–180, for a summary of those important dates.

Meeting with the School Counselor

Most school counselors are familiar with the colleges and training programs that exist in your area, and they will often have a sense of what might be a good fit for your teen. Even in this budget-challenged age, when counselors are stretched thin and expected to assist huge numbers of students, they can be enormously helpful to you and your child. Even if your teen's counselor doesn't know him well, you and/or your teen should still make an appointment to discuss your student's interests, goals, and needs. The vast knowledge counselors have of schools and financial aid programs makes them a valuable resource.

If you have good relationships with teachers and school counselors, those relationships can benefit your child in the long run. You can ask questions for your teen and, more importantly, direct your teen to the help that is available. This is where the balance between advocating for your child and teaching him independence begins to shift.

School counselors at many high schools meet with each senior individually during the first half of the school year.

Students often schedule their own meetings, but the counselor does seek out those who don't make appointments on their own. The advantage to a student-scheduled appointment is that the student can do it early in the process, asking valuable questions she can later follow up on through college visits or other forms of research. Encourage your teen to get to know his counselor in the early years of high school. Often it is the counselor who can help him select the courses he will need to match his interests and goals.

One school counselor has shepherded hundreds of students through this process. She works with a wide range of students: from teens suspended from regular school programs who need alternative ways to earn a high school degree to kids planning to attend community and junior colleges to others who set their sights on elite universities. From her perspective, one of the best things parents can do is let their children "own" their own search process.

Listening to Your Teens and Letting Them Do the Legwork

One way parents can foster teens' independence in the search process is by really listening to them. Psychiatrist William Glasser, a psychotherapist and human behavior specialist, says there are four ways to interact with children: doing things for them, to them, with them, and leaving them alone. One school counselor who agrees with Glasser says that we don't do enough of the latter two with teens. And as children hit their late teens, these two become the most necessary. This counselor says:

Visit colleges with them. Spend time over dinner, go out for coffee, listen to them. Be available as a sounding board. Give them time to talk about what they are going through and thinking. I know, they won't always feel like talking, but keep creating opportunities. There is a lot to process and even if they don't know it, they need to talk about what is going on in their minds and hearts.

She adds, "Don't do the legwork for them," and emphasizes that the legwork is mostly online. Thoroughly researching post–high school options can now be done reliably this way. Your student needs to learn to navigate available online systems and do her own research. In fact, everything from college registration to certain elements of coursework and electronic textbooks themselves requires a high level of comfort working online.

Contrasting Approaches to the Planning Process

This same school counselor shared several telling anecdotes. One was about a young woman from an impoverished family that moved often, sometimes living in temporary shelters. This young woman by necessity did all her own post–high school research and made use of the resources offered at her school. She took charge of planning her future and is now thriving at a community college, covering her tuition with a partial scholarship and a part-time job.

A second teen applied to 15 colleges. However, his mother filled out each application and even used her name as the online user ID. This young man was accepted by some schools, but had a very hard time navigating even the course registration process because he had had so little practice doing things for himself. Once he was in college, he floundered.

A third, highly "enabled" student called home from campus on the first day of classes to say she couldn't find her way to her first class. Her mother phoned the admissions office and told a counselor that the counselor needed to help her daughter find her way to class. The counselor's response was "No, *you* need to come pick up your daughter. If she can't find her own way around campus, she isn't ready to be here."

Another wise school counselor advises parents to try hard not to project preconceived notions about the "right path" onto their teens. A four-year college simply isn't the right path for every student. Some just aren't ready for college at 18, yet are pushed into it by well-meaning parents. They may end up dropping out during or after their first year. College may be the right option, however, at some later time. It's important to note that for those who don't feel ready or simply want a different life experience before committing to college, such a choice requires courage. It is hard to go against what most other people do. School counselors have a wealth of information available to offer students on junior college programs, vocational-technical schools, and service-oriented programs. For more on this subject, see Chapter 3, Exploring Work, Service, and Other Paths, page 33.

Ideally, high school students will set up meetings with their school counselor in the first, second, and third years of high school to ensure early on that they are on track with course selections that support the direction that interests them. Certainly by early fall of the final high school year your teen should have met with a school counselor.

Meeting with the counselor will provide the most value if your teen has done some research in advance. Then he'll be able to ask the counselor questions such as: "If I'm interested in becoming a teacher, which of the 10 schools I've done some reading about would be best for me? If my first choice is X, but my grade point average may not get me in, what would make a good second choice?" During the meeting, the school counselor should go over the application process with each student. The counselor's mission and job is to make clear what steps are involved and what resources are available. When this meeting takes place, have your student take notes.

Your school's counselors know when students must sign up for the Scholastic Aptitude Test (SAT) and the American College Test (ACT), and they will advertise those dates to students. You can also find test information and sample questions, test dates, locations, and other details at the testing companies' Web sites—www.collegeboard.com for the SAT and www.act.org for the ACT. (For a helpful date summary, see "A High School Time Line for Parents and Teens," page 175.)

Your teen will be able to indicate on the test registration forms the names of programs and colleges to which test scores should be sent. While your teen can have scores sent for one inclusive price to several schools upon first taking the tests, it is worth considering sending scores initially to the home address and high school to give you and your teen a chance to evaluate the scores. For an additional fee, your son or daughter can send later the scores that he or she is happy with.

Encourage your student to do some of the necessary soul-searching and questioning early so that when she meets with her counselor, she can share her interests and abilities, and her dreams for the future. The school counselor is an excellent resource for helping to match future dreams with the practical steps needed to get there.

➤

Visiting the School's College and Career Center

Danielle Jastrow runs the college and career center at Southwest High School, an urban Minneapolis public school with roughly 2,000 students. The center is open to all students. It provides guidebooks, program admissions materials, and computers that students can use to research post–high school options and match their interests and abilities to available programs. Jastrow likes to remind parents that the vocational or college search involves helping teens find a good fit for themselves, and is not a prestige contest for parents. She quoted a colleague who believes the college and career search "is a match to be made, not a prize to be won." Jastrow's college and career center offers the online Naviance guidance program to students and families, finding it an extremely helpful tool to help match personality traits to available programs in a range of financial categories.

Jastrow begins working with teens in their freshman year. She periodically pulls them out of classes to meet and offer them interest inventories and assessments that allow students the chance to understand more about who they are, as well as learn more about their interests and abilities. Along with parent volunteers, the college and career center staff helps kids focus on the following questions, which can lead them to the next step that best suits their individual needs:

- Who are you now? Who do you see yourself becoming?
- What are your dreams and visions for the future?
- What activities would be satisfying or gratifying for you to be involved in?
- What would you like to contribute to the world?

As Jastrow tells teens, "It's not about *where* you go . . . it's about what you do when you get there."

The application process officially begins in the fall of senior year, but it is smart for your teen to do some of the research in the junior year or even earlier. Significantly, Jastrow begins her work with students when they first enter high school. This early start is invaluable as, with her help, teens can begin to explore and articulate who they are and where they are headed, and can be confident that the courses they need to enroll in and the tests they need to take will move them in the direction they identify for themselves.

Jastrow enlists parent volunteers to read drafts of students' college essays and help fine-tune them. She recommends that teens ask one of their best and most insightful resources—their English teacher—for help in writing college essays, reminding them that the greater the number of objective readers of their essays, the better. And about the essays themselves, Jastrow says, "It's not only about how well-written [they are], but it's also about 'voice.' Are students able to communicate, in writing, who they are and what makes them distinctive?"

Personal Interest Assessments and Career Inventories

The following personal interest assessments and career inventories are available to teens through school counseling offices and online. They can help students identify personal strengths and suggest career and educational areas that are compatible with those strengths.

- The online guidance program *Naviance* matches student interests to available opportunities and colleges (among its many other features). Students whose schools pay a subscription fee to Naviance can access the system free of charge (www.naviance.com).
- The *Strong Interest Inventory* (High School Edition) is given online and on paper. This assessment

takes about 40 minutes and is fee-based. It helps
a young person identify post-secondary options
that align with personal characteristics and lists
steps a student can take to sort through education
and career options. It also includes tips for parents
(www.skillsone.com).

- The *Self-Directed Search* is an interest and personality inventory that matches interests to potential
careers and was created by author and researcher
John Holland (see www.self-directed-search.com;
www.hollandcodes.com).

- The *Kuder Career Planning System* (Navigator) is
a college and career exploration assessment that
can be saved online in an electronic portfolio that
students can access over their lifetime and share
online (www.kuder.com).

Applying to Schools

*The application is an opportunity to shine. The students
who best demonstrate that they are motivated, eager
learners will make the biggest impact on admission committees. . . . Students should spend some time thinking
about who they are, what makes them special, and what
they hope to accomplish in college before sending in an
application.*

COLLEGES THAT CHANGE LIVES WEB SITE (www.ctcl.org)

Once your teen has done enough research to narrow the
choices, the application process begins in earnest. Some
school counselors recommend that teens apply for admission to as many as five to eight schools, identifying at least
one financial "safety school" among them—one that is real-
istically affordable given your family's situation.

One factor in the application process involves choosing a deadline that suits your teen. Some schools feature "rolling admissions," making admission decisions and sending acceptance and rejection letters on a continuous basis. Many more schools offer students two primary types of deadlines: Early Decision and Regular Decision. One advantage to both types of deadlines lies in timing. For students who are ready to apply to college early in their senior year, it makes sense to submit applications under Early Decision deadlines in the fall. For others who need more time to make up their minds or do additional research, Regular Decision deadlines after January 1 are the logical choice.

The application includes the actual application form and many of the following elements: test score reports (sent directly from the testing organization); one, two, or more personal essays; letters of recommendation from a school counselor and generally two teachers; and an official copy of the student's academic transcript (sent by the high school counseling office). Many colleges and universities use an online application form called the Common Application (often referred to as the Common App; see www.commonapp.org). The Common App forms the basis of the application, which some colleges also augment with an additional, required application form. Specific application requirements are available on each school's Web site.

While not all schools require students to submit a written essay, for those that do this is a crucial component. Beyond a well-written essay, admissions committees look for writing that illustrates what makes your student unique and well-suited to the school. The essay is worth an investment of time, thought, and energy, not only for the end result but also to help a student clarify and articulate who he is and what his goals are. For a listing of helpful essay-writing resources, see the Bibliography, page 181.

Our teen wrote an essay about the self-knowledge she gained during a challenging six-week canoe trip. A fairly confident writer, she still struggled to choose her angle of focus. Several drafts helped her clarify her themes: she had learned a lot about teamwork and getting through tough moments with her peers, continuing on to the other side with camaraderie and laughter. She also wrote of how the landscape sparked her interest in and passion for environmental issues.

Your student doesn't need an exotic anecdote to write a suitable admission essay. Themes of family, community, work, and academic challenge form the basis for many successful essays, and these are topics to which all teens have access. If your teen struggles to write an essay, and you feel the limitations of trying to coach and guide objectively, ask a friend or colleague who is an excellent writer to help your teen. Chances are that an objective reader will be far enough removed from the emotions of essay writing to offer an impartial yet supportive stance. Your teen may have fleshed out an essay that is still rough, and an objective reader can talk him through the holes, asking questions, providing encouragement, and helping your teen write with greater clarity.

It's critical that teens write their essays themselves. The qualities they bring to their essay writing are the qualities that they will take with them to college. Admissions counselors need to be able to see these qualities clearly. An objective reader's role is simply to help the writer refine and sharpen his focus. With final proofreading from you and others, chances are that your teen will accomplish his goals with his essay.

Letters of recommendation are another typical part of the application process. School counselors write letters of recommendation for every student based upon a general knowledge of a student's overall academic characteristics.

Many colleges ask for letters from teachers, especially those teaching core academic subjects (math, science, history, language arts) who can accurately address your teen's strengths and weaknesses.

Help your teen think through the list of teachers with whom she has established particular rapport, and who you believe would write favorably and knowledgeably about her. Remind her to ask early for a teacher's recommendation, giving a teacher advance notice—at least three weeks. It is a courtesy to teachers for teens to give them stamped, pre-addressed envelopes along with the school recommendation form, as well as a list of your teen's activities—even an activity résumé. Have your teen write thank-you notes to teachers and counselors to acknowledge their time and effort. See "The College Application Package," page 179, for a summary of all the application elements.

College Visits

Visiting college campuses can give your teen a feel for the kind of setting where she will be most comfortable. Sometimes students, including my own teen, visualize themselves living in a specific locale—in my daughter's case, a small campus far from the city. Making a few college visits helped my teen realize that the excitement of a larger campus was what she ultimately wanted, and this helped her narrow her choices. At times she also thought she would choose a distant destination, but she ended up going to a school only a four-hour drive away. It was far enough, but not too far. Not only did the school fit her criteria for a larger campus, it also offered excellent courses in her areas of interest. When she visited, she had really liked the "feeling" on campus, the students' enthusiasm for their surroundings and classes. According to one school counselor, it is often this feeling of connection to a place and a campus that makes for a strong, positive choice.

Some schools, communities, and service organizations offer students opportunities for low-cost group trips to colleges in various parts of the country. This makes college trips more affordable. Such opportunities also provide the camaraderie of friends in the research phase. Another money-saving idea is to carpool informally with other parents and kids to tour campuses of interest within driving distance. And by calling admissions offices in advance, you can easily set up organized tours for your teen and ensure that you can have your questions answered by tour guides and admissions officers. Schools are often willing to let students sit in on classes of particular interest to them, too, if you've given them time to contact professors and set up an itinerary.

It takes effort to dig into financial resources and set aside work and school schedules to visit potential schools and other post–high school options with teens. Yet I look back fondly on those trips with our teen. They were instrumental in helping her make good choices. We enjoyed fun, focused time together, just the two of us. Our schedule was often packed, but by evening, even school campuses quiet down. And sitting together at dinner, or on a train, bus, or plane, provided us with valuable talking time. Every trip, every expenditure, is underscored by daunting but exciting and fruitful questions for teens: Which is the best choice for me? Where will I fit? Where can I best prepare for my future, intellectually and experientially? How do I map out my future?

Portfolios and Auditions

If your student is considering a program in the arts, she may need to prepare a portfolio that best exhibits her work or prepare a selection for auditions. Putting together a port-folio usually requires a lot of help—the assistance of an art or photography teacher is ideal under these circumstances. Parents, too, are instrumental in this process, if for no other reason than providing moral support and buying needed supplies. Compiling a portfolio is a time-consuming pro-cess, definitely not a task to be put off until the last minute. (Art supply stores are most likely *not* open at midnight.) Portfolios are tangible proof of creative energy. Viewing the breathtaking paintings and sketches in the portfolio of one young woman, I was struck by how hard she had already been working in her field. Art school seemed to be the per-fect match for her passion and talent.

Some schools require photographic slides of artwork, especially work that is difficult to send by mail. How to best transmit your teen's work to potential schools will depend on the particular art form or medium. Each school has its own requirements and guidelines. You and your student can research those guidelines online or by reviewing admission forms you have received.

Auditions are another aspect of the admission process for schools or programs that focus on performing arts. Schools often require live auditions for musicians, dancers, and actors. So what happens when you live in Ohio and want to audition for a program in Oregon? A lot of schools provide opportunities for auditions at regional sites closer to home in an effort to spare families the sometimes prohibitive cost of travel. And quite a few schools also accept recorded audi-tions in place of live auditions.

Clearly the "closed door" audition defines the line that separates what parents can directly influence and direct and what they cannot. You may have found the right teacher or mentor; paid for lessons; listened or watched with rapt attention as your teen played or performed; supported her;

loved her; traveled with her; and walked her to the door. But what happens next after your teen crosses the threshold is up to her.

Waiting and Deciding

Stiff competition has left my friends and me on edge— wondering if we are "worthy" enough for admission to the colleges of our choice. Ideally, parents should be the even keel in this process, providing positive reinforcement and support.

MEREDITH BAKER, COLUMNIST FOR
THE *HOUSTON CHRONICLE,* OCTOBER 17, 2008

Decisions about their futures hang over teens' heads before and during the senior year and carry a palpable weight. Those who apply in the fall under a Rolling Admission or Early Decision deadline are spared some of the ongoing tension that accompanies the application preparation phase and colors the senior year. Most students, though, need additional time (and often, winter break) to sift through the options, make final visits, and complete applications. The tension that accompanies application preparation (writing essays, filling in paper and electronic forms, facing immutable deadlines) is followed by the uncertainty that accompanies the waiting period. Students hear from their colleges or other programs at different times, so all around them teens feel the anxiety and excitement of future plans being made or dismantled. Teens and parents watch mailboxes like never before.

As a parent of an older teen during this time, you may experience a natural and healthy progression away from your role as a guardian and a shift toward an advisory role and as a guide. Already it's possible that you sense the limits of even this role. If we become overly involved in our kids' choices, we lose the ability to center our family. A parent's most important role becomes our ability to offer guidance in the form of positive reinforcement and support while teens decide what their next steps will be.

And what does it mean to be a guide? Guides provide maps, and on this journey, teens have a need for both resource and emotional maps. For the former, parents can help guide teens to individuals and written sources for researching postsecondary options (of which there are an overwhelming number). Guiding teens emotionally means being aware on a deep level of this almost seismic passage young people are embarking upon.

I found it helpful to be consciously aware of this process—seeing the big picture—and to ask questions from time to time about how my child was feeling, even just occasionally saying, "This is a big year, isn't it? How are you handling the pressure?" Sometimes the larger focus is simply forgotten as the need to focus on deadlines and events overtakes the daily routine.

Keeping Things in Perspective

Ultimately, where your student chooses to attend college doesn't matter so much as the energy and enthusiasm they bring to their experience.

COLLEGES THAT CHANGE LIVES WEB SITE

One parent commented on the applications period surrounding her second teen's senior year, "I had to keep hounding him about college applications. I tried to get him to do them over the summer so we weren't running around like chickens with our heads cut off at the last minute, but he didn't want to—in part because he didn't *have* to yet."

She added wryly, "Of course, there's always going to be some of that."

A veteran of the process and mother of three, she'd been through this once already and knew some of the challenges that lay ahead. The hard part for her was to keep coming up with the energy to advise and prod, in the midst of her own job and caring for her family. The second time around, she had the advantage of prior experience and the knowledge of the sometimes exhausting demands of the process. "It just helped to acknowledge all the work involved," she says. "Most other parents nodded their heads if I said it out loud. I had to rest sometimes, give myself a break."

Another mom whose son (and first senior in the family) is now in college looks back on the final high school year and wishes she had worried less. "There's so much hype and hoopla about colleges and applying and getting in, and I got caught up in it. In truth he, in his own quiet way, did research online, and we visited a few colleges. He applied to several and was accepted by his top choice. I worried. I fretted. I nagged. I could have done less of all of that."

Early Decision, Early Action, Rolling Admission, and Regular Admission Deadlines

Unfortunately, getting in to college sometimes feels like trying to fit 10 boats through a narrow channel in the river. Inevitably, only one can get through at a time. This trend is true across the board—state universities that 10 years ago were often considered back-up schools now turn down solid students. I say this not to further feed the frenzy, but to shed light on why teens feel so much pressure and why the process is nerve-racking for all involved. One mistake—a missed deadline, a typographical error in a college admission essay—and you may be thrown overboard.

Sam Dillon, writing for the *New York Times*, says, "The brutally low acceptance rates this year were a result of . . . a demographic bulge (that) is working through the nation's population—the children of baby boomers are graduating from high school in record numbers. . . . Another factor is that more high school students are enrolling in college immediately after high school. . . . The third trend driving the frantic competition is that the average college applicant applies to many more colleges than in past decades" (April 4, 2007). Fortunately, not all schools and programs are obsessively competitive, and excellent schools and programs abound. See the Bibliography, page 181, for several resources describing underappreciated gems.

Many colleges and universities offer a series of staggered application deadlines for admission to the following year's class. Applying for early admission through Early Decision or Early Action can give qualified students the advantage of competing against a smaller application pool and potentially receiving an admission offer before the normal deluge of applications arrives for consideration at admission offices over the winter break. This option works well for students who have a clear idea about where they would most like to go to school. But it is wise to prepare backup applications to other schools as well. In this process, putting all of your eggs into one basket is too risky.

Seniors who apply for Early Decision or Early Action must send in their applications by September or October, which means they must have taken their college entrance exams (the SAT, ACT, and any SAT II tests) by the end of their junior year. Early Decision and Early Action acceptance letters, denials, and "wait lists" are sent in December of the senior year. If your student receives an Early Decision acceptance letter, he must agree to attend that college and withdraw any other pending applications. An Early Action acceptance does not require a student to commit to that school.

The beauty of an Early Decision acceptance is that halfway through the senior year, while other students are madly filling out applications, writing essays, and sweating bullets over the decision ahead, your student may know already where she is headed. But Early Decision only works for a small percentage of students. Most apply to multiple colleges, and it only becomes clear as they move through their senior year which one feels most right to them. Key factors are the acceptance-denial process and financial aid packages. So choices and decisions unfold over time.

Rolling Admission schools don't establish just one set deadline; instead, they usually review applications throughout the year. The earlier in the academic year your child applies to Rolling Admission schools, the better his chances for acceptance. Our own teen applied in the fall to a Rolling Admission school. It was a happy day when she received the acceptance—her first. Bounding up the stairs, she called ecstatically, "Mom, Dad! I got accepted!" She sat at the end of our bed and read the letter aloud. I watched her, bright-eyed, enthusiastic, and perched on the edge of her future. I could almost imagine her sprouting wings and flying happily out of the room. At the time, this school wasn't her first choice, but its acceptance letter provided her with a great deal of comfort in the weeks ahead.

Over the next few months she heard from other schools. While she was turned down by her first choice, it didn't matter in the end. By late April she had decided to visit the first school that had accepted her, and fell in love there with the place and its energy. So she ended up quite happily at the school that had won her heart. The irony is that, as thrilled as she had been with her first acceptance, she had seen it only as her backup, until at the last moment it moved into first place.

Stepping Beyond the Family Path

Eric moved to the United States from Mexico with his family when he was 5 years old. He learned English and excelled in school. Several teachers took a special interest in Eric, and his parents were proud and supportive of his studies, although they did not have formal educational experience to share with him. However, he says of his parents, "They were *always* there to listen to me." The results of a career inventory assessment he took showed that Eric was consistently drawn to the health care field. He had always been fascinated with the way the human body works.

Eric had long talks with his father's cousin, a doctor, about his work. Although only one of Eric's five older siblings had gone to college, Eric saw himself as a trailblazer for the family, and described himself as "hungry." He wanted to help others, and he knew he eventually wanted to go medical school. But college first—and that couldn't happen without a scholarship. His good grades and effort paid off. The day the college scholarship letter arrived, he said his "whole family got happy!" Eric reached beyond the accomplishments of everyone else in his immediate family. His parents continue to be proud and supportive of his efforts, and this helps him as he continues on his focused path.

The admissions process itself, as prolonged as it is, often becomes a key part of what clarifies the post–high school decision for many. Months of effort go into choosing the right college. Research, college visits, applications, rejections and acceptances, financial aid packages, and personal choice are all tributaries that feed into the same stream. When the decision is finally made, be sure to celebrate it with your teen. The hard work, effort, and lessons learned along the way are an important part of preparing for what lies ahead.

COLLEGE DECISIONS TO EXPLORE WITH YOUR TEEN

➤ How does your ideal school compare in size to your high school? Do you think you'd like a large school or a small school?

➤ How important is the school's geographic location to you? Is living close to a city or in a rural area important to you?

➤ What major areas of study interest you?

➤ What do you imagine yourself doing to earn a living or contribute to the world?

➤ Does the school offer or excel at the kinds of programs and courses you want to take?

➤ Does the school have extracurricular activities that are important to you?

➤ What kind of school is financially feasible when you add in travel costs?

➤ What is financially doable for the family? (This isn't always obvious until a financial aid offer is made by a school.)

➤ Do you have at least one financial safety school on your list?

➤ What place *feels* like the right place for you? Where do you sense a connection to the students, place, coursework, and professors?

CHAPTER 5

Money, Money, Money: Learning to Handle It Wisely

Management of money often becomes an arena for the independence struggle.

KAREN LEVIN COBURN AND MADGE LAWRENCE TREEGER,
*LETTING GO: A PARENTS' GUIDE TO
UNDERSTANDING THE COLLEGE YEARS*

One of the primary reasons to be clear about how much you can afford and are willing to help your child financially is that it makes it less likely that money will become a weapon you use to get your child to do what you want. Few teens can afford to be completely independent financially. When you are honest about your own financial situation, you set the stage for negotiating your teen's financial dependence on you in a respectful way. Working together closely also allows teens and parents to make steady progress toward their eventual financial independence. If you use money as a tie to bind your teen to you and your will, you shortchange him in the process.

Hold an honest and open discussion about what you can afford and what your teen must pay over the coming year. Obviously, a huge part of becoming a fully independent person is developing financial responsibility. Ask your teen, "Do you really need a particular item or do you just want it? Do you already have the money to pay for it? If not, how can you save what you'll need to purchase it?" It's worth taking the time to sort through true needs and wants and to back up your findings with a little research.

Money 101—Setting Up a Budget

A well-constructed budget will help you both clarify spending goals and make reasonable plans. While your teen may not know exactly what size allowance she'll need for food, transportation, entertainment, and personal expenses, one way to figure this out is to have her track her expenditures for an entire month. A monthly budget is a part of life, no matter where your teen lives. Help him set up a budget that includes entertainment expenses, transportation, fuel, insurance costs that he'll be responsible for, rent, utilities, cell phone bills, clothing, and any other expenses he will need to pay you or a landlord. Together, identify additional budget items as accurately as you can. Note that decisions like taking a year off before college, working full time or part time while in school, or volunteering with a service organization all affect your teen's financial situation in some way.

If your teen plans to attend college, suggest that she talk with college students she knows to find out what expenses they incur, or ask parents of current college students what spending amounts are realistic in particular settings. Expenses will vary from campus to campus, setting to setting, and student to student. Schools themselves often offer students suggested budgets, which is helpful since prices fluctuate by location. Once your teen is on campus, he will find that many colleges and universities subscribe to the National Endowment for Financial Education's (NEFE) Web site for students, www.cashcourse.org. The site offers many financial literacy tools free to students.

Opening a Checking Account

If you haven't done so already, help your teen set up her own checking account during her senior year (or certainly in the summer after graduation). Teach your teen how to write a check (even though she won't be writing many in this era of bank and debit cards). Make sure she knows to keep a driver's license or ID card nearby in order to cash a check. Encourage her to make regular deposits in her account. If she has a job, find out if direct deposit is an option. Have your child set aside a fixed amount of money to pay her bills each month. This is a useful practice, whether money comes from a summer job or is transferred from a college savings fund.

The discipline of balancing a checkbook (or managing an online account) is a big part of becoming financially independent. While students use fewer and fewer checks, it's important that your teen still regularly balance expenditures against account balances, remembering that while electronic bank transactions take effect within a day or so, not all withdrawals (or deposits) are instantly reflected in an online bank balance. Teens need to get in the habit of regularly checking their account balances and can easily do so from a computer or cell phone.

Help your teen set up overdraft protection in order to cover potential overdrafts, especially in the early months of check card use, check writing, ATM withdrawals and fees, and automatic account withdrawals. No longer do bounced checks arrive days later in the mail. When teens aren't paying attention, they can easily incur several fees for a single "insufficient funds" mistake—a real double whammy that may end up costing hundreds of dollars. Bank fees can easily top $60 or more per overdraft item. Do try to be understanding if your teen overdraws an account a few times in the first year of independent living. It's all part of the learning curve.

How One Family Handled Budgets and Credit

When her children were in middle school, Celia and her husband worked out a budget system with their children. By the time the kids reached high school, they were allowed to use the family credit card for some budgeted purchases. When the credit card statement arrived each month, Celia and her husband had their children circle and initial their charges. If someone's charges exceeded the allowed budget amount, it had to be repaid. This system worked for Celia. She says it succeeded because she was very clear about what she and her husband would and would not pay for. When her teens left home, their budget was effectively in place.

Early on, Celia consulted a few parents whose children had left home and were living on their own. She asked about the allowance and budget amounts they had considered reasonable, and let those numbers guide her as she, her spouse, and their teens created realistic budgets. She spoke to one family whose college-age teens were required to work during the summer, saving at least half their earnings to cover college textbook purchases and personal expenses.

Another family decided they didn't want their daughter to use her college's universal campus card—a debit card typically loaded by parents with part of the room-and-board fee—to pay for her laundry, meals, and other campus-related expenses. They knew that it was sometimes all too easy to ignore a dwindling balance on a campus card. Instead, the parents asked their daughter to use cash from her bank account for her meals and other expenditures so that she could plainly see where her money was going and how quickly ordinary spending reduced her balance. These parents set a limit on the amount of money they were willing to give their daughter, and they expected her to stick to her budget.

Using Online Budgeting Tools

Many teens are quite technologically savvy and may find online budgeting tools to be helpful. Budget tracking can help a teen realize how much and on what he is spending each month. This useful tool can also help parents set a reasonable allowance for kids and decide what expenses you will and will not cover.

Mint.com is a free budgeting site that allows the user to track average spending in certain categories (food, laundry, movies). An e-mail or text-message alert is sent to the user when he is close to the budget limit. Mint.com can also alert you to low account balances, hopefully preventing the account from becoming overdrawn. Other free financial management Web sites providing similar services include Wesabe.com and Geezeo.com. Quicken.com provides a free trial period and then charges a monthly fee for its online financial management tools.

Understanding Credit Cards, Reports, and Scores

Karen Levin Coburn and Madge Lawrence Treeger note in their book *Letting Go: A Parents' Guide to Understanding the College Years* that "credit card companies are courting college students—with great success for the companies and devastating results for many students." A university representative at our teen's freshman orientation remarked, "We don't recommend credit cards for first-year students. We have known so many who get in way over their heads."

Eighteen-year-olds are faced with profound changes in their lives when they first leave home, and the allure of a line of credit is often more than many are ready to handle. It's too easy to use credit spending as a cover for the lost and lonely feelings that may surface when a young person is first finding his or her way in the world. It's also tempting to charge tuition and other college expenses and rack up high-interest debt quickly.

The timetable for responsibly using credit cards differs for each person. Some teens are developmentally ready to use credit cards reliably in high school. When our daughter was in her third year of college she obtained her first credit card. By then, she had successfully handled her own financial affairs for some time. She was heading out of the country for a semester and needed a credit card for some travel expenses. We emphasized the importance of paying the credit card balance on time to avoid an interest charge.

Teens often don't realize that their credit card payment history will be tracked electronically by three national credit bureaus (Experian, TransUnion, and Equifax) for *many* years. Explain to your teen that all credit and consumer account payments—on-time payments, late payments, and nonpayments of credit card bills, student loans, rent, utilities, and other charges—are recorded each month. This payment record forms the basis of a person's overall credit record and credit score. Teens should know that they can incur a poor credit score from making late rental, utility, car, and credit payments, having maxed-out credit accounts, and other factors, making it impossible to be eligible for future car loans, apartment rentals, mortgage approval, various kinds of insurance, other credit cards, and sometimes certain jobs. For more information, see the National Endowment for Financial Education's consumer financial resources at www.smartaboutmoney.org.

Your teen can build a positive credit history by paying bills on time and avoiding debt. Let your teen know that one way to establish a positive credit history is to apply for one credit card, use it to make one purchase, pay the balance promptly, and then tuck it away for emergency use only. Once she's established a good credit history, she can check it for accuracy by obtaining a free credit report once a year. For more information, see the Federal Trade Commission's Web site, www.ftc.gov/freereports.

Modeling Good Financial Habits

Many of us learned our most basic money lessons by trial and error, through observing our parents and watching our peers. You have the opportunity to teach your teen realistic money management strategies that will last a lifetime. Be honest, if you can, in discussing the parameters of your own financial situation—its possibilities and limitations. The abilities to earn, save, and spend money wisely are important skills teens need to learn on the road to adulthood. Somewhere between shepherding your teen along the financial learning curve and expecting him to treat money maturely is the sweet spot—the steady progression of financial understanding. Help your teen value the importance of working toward financial goals, and use sales, comparison shopping, and coupons as your allies.

Making wise financial decisions is a huge piece of what parents can teach and model to children. Even if your own financial decisions haven't always been the best, share lessons learned from past mistakes and be candid about what you might have done differently. If you don't feel qualified to teach financial literacy to your teen, ask for financial advice and reliable information for yourself and your teen from a trusted banker or financial adviser.

GETTING FINANCIALLY FIT

➤ Figure out a budget with and for your teen. Hold your teen responsible for sticking to the budget.

➤ Be consistent in the money messages you send your teen.

➤ Have your teen try an online budgeting and financial management tool such as mint.com, quicken.com, wesabe.com, geezeo.com, or others to practice budgeting over time and working toward financial goals.

➤ Talk to your teen about responsible use of credit cards. Together, decide when (or if) it's appropriate to use a credit card. For additional resources, see NEFE's consumer Web site, www.smartaboutmoney.org.

➤ Show your teen an actual credit report, if you have one. You can request one free report per year at www.ftc.gov/freereports. Your teen can do the same once she establishes a credit record through her prompt payment history.

➤ Help your teen understand how credit scores are calculated and the impact credit scores have by visiting credit scoring company Fair Isaac's Web site, www.myfico.com. There is a fee for ordering a personal credit score report.

CHAPTER 6

Navigating the Financial Aid Maze

There's no doubt about it: children are expensive—all along the way—and the ante only goes up when it comes to higher education expenses. Perhaps you've been setting aside savings for college tuition since your child was born, or maybe you plan to take tuition expenses out of your current paycheck, hoping that in this way you can partially or completely cover the ever-rising costs of college. Some parents may be able to help with education expenses, but also need their child to contribute to the costs by working part or full time.

Navigating the financial aid maze is a necessity for many families who want to get children successfully through school. Some students manage to pay for college entirely on their own, but this feat has become harder and harder to achieve. An unfortunate outcome of tuition increases over the years is that a high percentage of college students leave school owing a good deal of money. The issue requires some soul-searching from parents: How much are we willing and able to help out?

A mistake some parents make is helping their children financially to the detriment of their own financial security. The following example might be considered a worst-case scenario: the parents of one teen went so deeply into debt in order to put their daughter through the school of her choice that they eventually needed to sell the family home to cover their financial obligations. The young woman had no idea how overextended her parents had become. In the end, the parents did both themselves and their daughter a disservice. While there are many, *many* ways to pay for college, bankruptcy should not be one of them. Even if your ability to help pay your child's education expenses is limited, your child should know the truth of the matter so he can understand your financial limits. This is a conversation that parents and children must have early in the college search process.

Financing Your Child's Higher Education

Families work out the school finance equation in a million different ways—from being completely "hands off" ("You'll have to find your own way to pay for college") to offering a child a fully financed college fund set up in advance. But there are lots of variations in between these extremes. Often, it comes down to forming working partnerships with teens ("You get the best grades you can and save your earnings; we'll see how much my job, your job, and financial aid will provide").

Whatever arrangements you work out, be honest and clear with your student and keep your word. It helps if you have figured out a specific amount you are willing and able to contribute along the way. But even if you haven't, you *can* come up with a budget for yourself and your student. This requires a particular kind of personal honesty. Admitting your financial limitations can be difficult, but it is *the* central reality of many, many lives. Being clear about what you expect from your child helps a teen make better choices and plan accordingly.

As financial advisers are quick to point out, student loans may be relatively easy to come by, but there is no such thing as a loan for a parent's retirement account. Instead of borrowing against your own future as the couple mentioned previously chose to do, take time to plan a strategy that works for your family. Gather college financing information from your teen's school counselor, search for information online, and call financial aid counselors at the schools you and your child like as possibilities.

Contrasting Family Approaches to Financing Education

One family agreed to pay for their children's first two years of college; the kids were on their own after that. The students knew upfront that they had to save hard-earned money, find scholarships, and/or arrange loans for their remaining under-graduate years. Another family agreed to pay all costs related to tuition and room and board, but their teen was respon-sible for the costs of textbooks, entertainment, meals outside the meal plan, and travel home for breaks and holidays. No matter what solution your family chooses, each comes with pros and cons, as well as a learning curve.

A student whose parents were divorced said his mom and dad argued incessantly about whose turn it was to help him financially throughout his college years; they argued over the specific amount as well. He could never count on having money reliably deposited in his college account. For students, the stress of not knowing how much financial help is available and when or if it will show up becomes a tremen-dous burden. If you can set up and stick to a consistent and honest financial arrangement with your child, you will create the healthiest situation for all.

Saving for Higher Education

Federal and state governments set up numerous investment plans to help families save money for post–high school education. Each option has its advantages and disadvantages, and each may have a specific impact on your student's eligibility for financial aid. What follows is a very basic overview and breakdown of some of the more well-known savings options. You can get more detailed information from the Internal Revenue Service's Web site at www.irs.gov.

It makes sense to set up the following savings plans so that you can accrue interest and use your money most effectively. Most government-sponsored plans allow you to save money that is "tax-deferred," meaning that you don't pay tax on the money until you actually withdraw it for education expenses and the government considers any interest income tax-free if you use it for education expenses (within certain parameters for valid education expenses and limits on a parent's income). Note that some income limits and maximum investment and withdrawal amounts in the government-sponsored savings plans may change over time. Check with a financial adviser for the best ways to match your particular situation to a savings plan suited to your needs.

529 Savings Plans

529 savings plans are state-sponsored college savings plans or college-sponsored prepaid tuition plans (also known as qualified tuition plans). Although plans vary slightly from state to state, 529 plans allow for tax-free distributions (which means that you "distribute" or withdraw the money, along with any earned interest) up to the amount that you pay for college tuition, books, fees, class supplies, and a

designated room and board amount. To be eligible for a tax break, you must provide proof that in the same year you withdraw money from your 529 plan, you also pay out that same amount in qualified expenses. Another advantage to having a 529 plan is that the investor (the parent, grandparent, or other qualified adult) remains in control of the money. You'll find an extensive discussion of 529 plans, with state-by-state comparisons, at www.savingforcollege.com.

Savings Bonds and Certificates of Deposit

You can purchase savings bonds and certificates of deposit (CDs) at a bank. Some employers also offer a payroll-deduction option for EE savings bonds. You can use the interest earnings on savings bonds and CDs as part of your college savings strategy. For families with incomes below a federally determined threshold, EE education savings bonds have the advantage of accruing tax-free interest when the proceeds are used for education-related expenses. Both of these investments are secure and designed for long-term investing; interest earnings are low but you will not lose money. Interest earnings on savings bonds are considered tax-deferred until you cash them.

Coverdell Education Savings Account (ESA)

The Coverdell Education Savings Account (the new, improved version of the government's early "Education IRA") is a flexible investment account with a designated beneficiary (meaning you specify who will receive the proceeds) who is either under 18 or has special needs. Withdrawals from Coverdell ESAs are tax-free when used for education (subject to certain income limits). However, a Coverdell ESA may be limited by your use of the Hope Credit or the Lifetime

Learning Credit (see page 98 for more information). Check with a tax adviser for more specific information. You can invest $2,000 per child, per year, in these accounts. Under Coverdell rules, families of soldiers killed in the line of duty may contribute, subject to certain limitations, up to 100 percent of the survivor benefits to a Coverdell ESA. Find out more at www.irs.gov and at www.savingforcollege.com.

UTMA / UGMA Accounts

The Uniform Transfers to Minors Act (UTMA) and Uniform Gifts to Minors Act (UGMA) allow an adult to give a gift of money to a child under age 18 up to a specified amount per year without being subject to gift taxes. Any amount above the gift threshold is taxed at the account custodian's rate (the adult responsible for the account). Taxes on interest earnings are assessed at a child's tax rate (which depends on the child's age and total income for the year). In general, a portion of the annual investment amount is either set off against the child's annual deduction or is taxed at the child's rate.

Ownership of UTMA/UGMA savings accounts transfers from the owner (typically the parent) to the beneficiary (typically the student) when the beneficiary turns 18 or 21, depending on how the account is set up. If you decide to set up an UTMA or UGMA account, you must be comfortable with the idea of giving your child ownership of the money at a designated point. Many parents think twice about this investment option for that very reason. Hillary Chura notes in the *New York Times* that "giving large sums to the future student is unwise for another reason. In determining college aid, the portion of money expected to go for college is higher for funds held in a student's hands than if it were the parents' money" ("Cracking the Books for Financial Aid to College," January 27, 2007). See www.finaid.org for an extensive discussion of UTMA and UGMA considerations. You'll want to be familiar with the following items if you and your student plan to apply for financial aid.

The FAFSA: Portal to Financial Assistance

When it comes to financial aid, everything begins with the FAFSA—the Free Application for Federal Student Aid. No matter what their financial situation, all students are eligible to submit an application at www.fafsa.ed.gov or by mail. The FAFSA is the key that opens the door to all federal aid possibilities, as well as to most financial aid from colleges themselves.

As a parent, I was filled with a quaking fear when I first learned about the form. It was one of those acronyms that, when spoken, seemed to set people off. "Oh, the FAFSA!" I heard other parents exclaim, and their heads would shake, brows would furrow, and knowing looks would be exchanged. Rumors trickled out from parents of older kids who had filled out the dreaded form. It sounded so daunting. The good news is that by filing the FAFSA, your student is automatically considered for all federal grants and loans, and for some of an individual school's scholarships.

As a newcomer to the FAFSA experience, I found the concept mysterious; I worried that the entire realm of financial aid would be impenetrable, or, at the very least, challenging to navigate. Tamar Lewin noted in the *New York Times*, "It [the FAFSA form] has become so intimidating—with more than 100 questions—that critics say it scares off the very families most in need" ("The Big Test Before College? The Financial Aid Form," February 21, 2009). The FAFSA is indeed intimidating, but once I got around to putting all the data in place, I found the task manageable.

The most time-consuming part is gathering the required

information. The FAFSA asks for income data found on W-2 income tax forms. Whether you do your own taxes or have a tax preparer fill them out, completing your tax returns first will enable you to submit a finalized FAFSA form. It is possible to use preliminary data and submit the FAFSA online or by mail beginning January 1 for the following school year; however, you will need to return and finalize the form in order to be considered for aid. For many parents, it seems to work best to prepare your income taxes as soon as possible after you receive W-2s and other tax information (usually by early February).

Note that when you file the FAFSA online, you will need personal identification numbers (PINs) for yourself and for your student; they can be obtained at www.pin.ed.gov. These PIN numbers are required in order to electronically "sign" the FAFSA. Before you file the FAFSA, first apply for the PIN numbers, allowing one to three days to receive them by e-mail. For more information, see the financial aid resources in the to-do list at the end of this chapter.

The FAFSA form becomes more complicated if you own a family business, have investment dividends, or receive gains from stocks in the past year. You are required to report all sources of income and business assets on the FAFSA. Primary home ownership and home market value are *not* factors in FAFSA student aid determination, nor are individual retirement accounts. The form does ask about your student's income.

Many colleges and some high schools offer free informational meetings and sometimes personal assistance in filling out the FAFSA. In addition, the U.S. Department of Education offers free workshops on the FAFSA. See www.fafsa.ed.gov for more information. There are also for-profit services available online that can provide assistance in filling out your forms.

According to writer Hillary Chura, families who think they won't need or qualify for financial aid should still consider filing the application "because they may have extenuating circumstances, like several children in college at the same time, that will make aid officers look on them more favorably" ("Cracking the Books for Financial Aid to College," *New York Times*, January 27, 2007).

Another reason to apply regardless of circumstances is that a family's economic situation can change dramatically over the course of an academic year, but the final FAFSA deadline is firm. If your situation changes, you won't have the option of filing the application late. But once you've submitted the FAFSA application, you do have the option of going back to your saved form and making alterations as your situation changes.

Besides filling out the FAFSA online, you can write to the Department of Education to request forms by mail (see the financial aid resources in the to-do list at the end of this chapter). Individual school FAFSA deadlines may vary from state to state and institution to institution; they range from early March to the start of the fall term.

Once you've completed the form, you will receive a notification of your family's Expected Family Contribution (EFC) on a Student Aid Report (SAR), which schools use to help determine the amount of financial aid they offer prospective students. The earlier you file the form, the more financial aid will be available, from both the federal government and individual schools. The EFC figure gives you an approximate idea of the amount you and your student will need to come up with above and beyond financial aid. The FAFSA is your child's ticket to scholarships and loans. Do yourself and your student a favor and make time to get it done well in advance of the deadline.

The financial aid offer you receive from a school will take

into account your EFC, as well as the school's own resources, and will either accompany your child's acceptance letter or follow it within a few weeks, depending upon the institution. Once you receive and assess the financial aid offer, you can decide what portion of the aid package you will accept. Your decision will be based, in part, on how much you are willing and able to help your teen.

Applying for Scholarships and Grants

Your teen can apply for a variety of scholarships through high school programs, foundations, service organizations, and college-specific programs. A scholarship may be part of an acceptance offer from a college. Merit-based scholarships are offered to high-performing students in academics, athletics, and the arts. Financial need–based scholarships are sometimes available; again, these rely on completion of the FAFSA. Most schools administer merit-based and need-based scholarships from sources such as alumni gifts and endowments, although some have more to offer than others. Competition is tough, but it's worth the effort that your teen musters to apply for any and all scholarships that seem to fit.

Many underpublicized scholarships exist. Since national scholarships are highly competitive, school counselors encourage students to be vigilant and creative when it comes to seeking out and applying for potential scholarships and grants. Free online resources that can help in this search include www.finaid.org, www.actstudent.org, and www.collegeboard.com. The Internet is a great tool; remember that you don't have to pay for scholarship information.

Investigate whether you or your student belongs to an organization that offers scholarships. Students are often eligible for scholarship aid from unions, fraternal organizations such as Lions Clubs and Rotary Clubs, faith-based groups, and businesses for which parents and students work. Look at your teen's extracurricular interests. Is your senior really into judo? Check it out. Perhaps aid is available from a philanthropic source committed to furthering the martial arts. Be sure to use the Internet as a search vehicle, and don't forget to talk to people involved in your student's areas of interest.

If your teen belongs to a minority group (ethnic, racial, ability, family, or personal status), it is worth looking for some of the many scholarships available to specific minority populations. The Gates Millennium Scholars Program (www.gmsp.org) provides "full ride" scholarships to qualified Black, Latina/Latino, American Indian, and Asian and Pacific Islander students. See the financial aid resources in the to-do list at the end of this chapter for more online scholarship links.

Athletic Scholarships

Athletic scholarships are highly competitive. If your student is a high school athlete, he may qualify for a partial or full scholarship depending upon a school's needs and your teen's abilities. Scholarship requirements differ and depend on whether your child is interested in a Division I, II, or III school (schools are classified according to number of students). If your teen hopes to play a Division I or II college sport, he will need to complete the NCAA Initial-Eligibility Clearinghouse Form, which will be mailed upon request to a student when the sixth semester (three years) of high school has been completed. It is best to complete this form at the beginning of the senior year, in August or September.

High school coaches are an important link to information for any teen who is interested in playing a club team sport or an NCAA sport in college. Strict rules govern when teens and college coaches can contact each other. College coaches often scout prospects early on through sports skills camps and summer programs for individual sports. Most often they are not allowed to scout student athletes at high school games.

If your child is interested in a specific college team, the more he or she knows about it, the better the advantage. Visiting college campuses to watch teams in action and meet some of the players can be a definite bonus. Even if a coach actively recruits your teen, remember that students still need to be accepted by the college's admission office. This means that grades and test scores are important. When your child is seriously considering a college choice based on an athletic decision, it is fair to ask the college coach many questions. As part of the application package, student athletes commonly record themselves in action and send coaches DVDs featuring their athletic abilities.

Many details factor in to receiving an athletic scholarship offer. Each school and sport differs slightly in its scholarship requirements. If your teen is athletically gifted, know that the competition is tough. Get as much information and help out of your high school coaches as you possibly can.

Arts Scholarships

Scholarships may be available to your student in music, dance, and other visual and performing arts. To be eligible for a music performance scholarship, your teen will need to contact music departments in advance and set up auditions. Plan for audition trips, either to the school campus or to a regional audition location. Your teen may also have the option of mailing an audition DVD to schools that are too far away to visit. Auditions and/or portfolios of creative work are a major component of applying for arts scholar-ships (see pages 65–67 for more information on auditions and portfolios).

Pell and FSEOG Federal Grants

Two government grant programs are the Federal Pell Grant and the Federal Supplemental Educational Opportunity Grant (FSEOG). Both of these grants are awarded on a financial-need basis determined by the financial aid office at your student's school. The grant amount is based on the information you submit on your FAFSA. Grants are gifts that do not have to be repaid. See www.ed.gov for more information.

Student Loans

Federal student loans include the Federal Perkins Loan Program (www.ed.gov) and the Federal Stafford Loan Program (www.staffordloan.com). The Perkins loan is a fixed-rate government loan; the loan amount is based on the financial need determined by a school's aid office and on the loan program's funds availability. Students can borrow a set amount per year up to a government-determined maximum. Interest and payments may be deferred for a specified period upon graduation or until the student is no longer enrolled at least half time.

Stafford loans come in two forms: subsidized and unsubsidized. Eligibility for the subsidized Stafford loan is based on need as determined by the financial aid office of a particular school and carries a fixed rate with annual and lifetime maximum limits for undergraduate work. The unsubsidized Stafford loan is not based on financial need (as determined by a school), although a limit applies to the amount you can borrow. A student cannot borrow more than the difference between the school's projected student costs and any other financial aid offer. The biggest difference between subsidized and unsubsidized Stafford loans is that interest accrues on unsubsidized Stafford loans while the student is still in school—in effect, as soon as the funds are disbursed.

Parent Loans

Federal Parent Loans for Undergraduate Students (PLUS loans) are available to parents from a variety of sources (typically banks) for children's college educations. Parents can borrow up to the amount needed to fund their child's education, minus the amount of other aid their student receives. The PLUS loan interest rate is variable and comes with a specified cap. Installment payments on PLUS loans begin 60 days after the loan money is disbursed, unless you apply for and receive a deferment. PLUS funds are paid directly to a college or university to cover tuition and other qualified expenses. If any funds are left over after all school fees have been paid, a refund is issued to you, the borrower.

➤ ────────────────────────────────────

One Borrower's Story

Bill borrowed money through the PLUS student loan program the first year his son was in college. The money did not come directly to him, but instead was disbursed from the loan-granting institution to the college bursar's office. Because Bill realized that the variable interest rate he received was not the deal he had originally thought it might be, he researched additional personal loans and found a private loan with a fixed interest rate that was as low as the one he had received on the variable-rate PLUS loan.

With the private loan coming directly to him, Bill was free in subsequent years to help his son not only with tuition, room, and board, but also with some travel expenses. The funds were his to direct at his own discretion, and he found this worked better for his needs. Bill had enough equity in his home and a strong employment history that made him eligible for the private loan. However, if the private loan had not been available as a backup, the PLUS loan might well have been his first choice.

Campus Work-Study Jobs

"Work-study" refers to a part-time job offer that is sometimes part of a college's financial aid package. Students may be awarded a certain amount of work-study aid that can be earned through a campus or community work-study job. Our daughter arranged a work-study internship at a small business close to campus that fit the scope of her studies and was willing to pay work-study wages. The work-study program is federally subsidized, so it becomes a good deal for employers, who pay half the employee's wages while the government pays the other half. This money comes in the form of a paycheck to the student. Your teen has direct control over work-study money in contrast to loan proceeds, which go directly to the bursar's office. Your teen can also choose to deposit work-study income directly with the college to pay for part of her school expenses.

Most campus jobs are work-study jobs. A student might wait tables at a campus café, staff the desk and shelve books in the library, or set up lighting for the theater. If your student is eligible for work-study, encourage him to look for work related to his interests or connected to his field of study. It is challenging to study *and* work, especially if a student is taking a full course load, but the time management and other skills a work-study job builds and the financial cushion it provides can be greatly beneficial.

Education Tax Credits and Deductions

The IRS offers two education tax credits to offset the costs of qualified education expenses. These education credits, the Hope Credit and the Lifetime Learning Credit, directly reduce the amount of income tax you pay and are based on your modified adjusted gross income. The Hope Credit is given to qualified wage earners for their college-age dependent student. It covers the student's first two years of higher education and is calculated on a per student basis. The Lifetime Learning Credit is calculated on a per family basis, with no limit to the number of years it can be claimed. This credit can be used for the qualified education expenses of both adults and children. Finally, interest you pay on student loans is also tax-deductible in certain circumstances. Check with a tax adviser about income limits and qualifications. For more information, see Publication 970, Tax Benefits for Education, at www.irs.gov/publications.

Regardless of the strategies you and your student devise to pay for higher education, it will be worth the effort. Whether you pay for school expenses from your current earnings, your student's savings, a combination of loans, grants, or other sources listed above, your teen will benefit in terms of increased earnings over the course of a lifetime if she or he gains the advanced training and education that you support.

FINANCIAL AID TO-DO LIST

➤ Be clear, honest, and thoughtful with your teen about how much you can help pay for college.

➤ Consider applying for financial aid—even if you don't think you'll qualify or need it—by filling out the FAFSA form and submitting it online at www.fafsa.ed.gov or by mail as soon as possible after January 1 of your teen's senior year.

➤ Submit the FAFSA to ensure that your child is in the running for federal grants and loans, work-study, and some scholarships. A free FAFSA guide is available in English and Spanish at www.studentaid.ed.gov (or call 800-433-3243 for more information).

➤ Encourage your teen to be creative in applying for scholarships. Scour newspapers, school newsletters, and your workplace for leads.

➤ Browse these Web sites for scholarship links and financial aid opportunities:

- Bankrate's Saving for College— www.savingforcollege.com

- FinAid: The SmartStudent™ Guide to Financial Aid— www.finaid.org

- Minnesota Office of Higher Education online resource page (includes national links in addition to those of regional interest)— www.getreadyforcollege.org

➤ Determine your need for loans to augment education savings plans you already have in place.

➤ Check with your tax or financial adviser about tax breaks associated with using education savings plans, investments, or loans for education expenses, and determine the best time and way to use these resources.

CHAPTER 7

Preparing Your Teen for Independent Living

We began to give our daughter more freedom, yet still expected her to communicate her basic schedule and whereabouts. It seemed like the right time for fewer rules, but steady communication [was also important].

FATHER OF A HIGH SCHOOL SENIOR

If she was coming home later than expected, I told my daughter to send me a text message. That way I could go to sleep. If I did wake up, I could check my phone to see what was going on with her.

MOTHER OF A NEW HIGH SCHOOL GRADUATE

"Intense" describes quite well the summer after high school graduation. Your teen may want to spend all her free time with high school friends. There will be several final get-togethers before teens scatter for summer work, school, and moves. Each movie, softball game, or bonfire—ordinary events in themselves—will take on a heightened, fleeting quality, and therefore seem less negotiable to your teen. However, parents still need sleep to function well the next day and may find the nights feeling longer. Preparing your teen to leave home, whether for college, work, or

> 101

service, will be one of the most intense family experiences for both of you. But it can also be an opportunity to work together and become closer.

Packing Up

While your teen packs, offer some mementos of home. In fact, when it comes to gifts that parents can send with a student who is moving out, family photos rank high. A special photo in a simple frame that captures a meaningful time can be a touchstone for your teen during some of the lonely moments ahead. New apartments and college dorm rooms abound with personal statements—it's part of how teens identify themselves to each other. Encourage your teen to pack a few treasured items, reminders of home and friends he is leaving.

I was touched by my daughter's choice of a photo of the two of us that she displayed on her dorm room desk. Nearby were special photos of her brother and of some particularly happy times the whole family had all shared over the summer. She and I spent good time together organizing her belongings for the big move. Her freshman dorm room had extra-long twin beds that required specially-sized sheets. Parents could order sheets from a supplier mentioned in the school's many mailings, but if she and I hadn't read the fine print on every piece of paper that arrived from the college, it would have been easy to miss this innocuous detail. I ordered two sets, but in retrospect realized one would have been plenty, for what student leaves sheets in the dryer overnight? Laundry is a one-day deal, and probably an infrequent one at that.

The Roommate Deal: Learning to Live with Others

Sharing a room with a complete stranger or a best friend (in a dormitory, apartment complex, or shared house) will inevitably be a lesson in accepting differences. Some teens will want to play music loudly and at all times; others prefer quiet in their room. Some are night owls and sleep late in the morning, while others are naturally early birds up at the crack of dawn. Sleep needs vary, and some can function well on four hours of sleep, while others can't make it without eight. Some need quiet, while others are more social, combining study with drop-in guests. Some are open to having visitors spend the night and others aren't. Some make their beds every morning, and others drop clothes and paperwork on the floor as they go. And these roommate differences are just the beginning.

Roommate relationships work on many different levels. Ideally, respect for differences evolves, as well as an agreement to respect separate social lives. At times a lifelong friendship begins. Sometimes the situation clearly does not work, and one roommate decides to move out. There are exceptions, but for most people, some issues will arise and have to be negotiated in one way or another. Sharing a living space is a character-building opportunity, and although it is intense, it is not unlike differences that will need to be worked out in future living and working situations.

This time can be a great opportunity for your teen to discover what's important to him, to take responsible care of himself, and to practice the art of compromise. Encourage your teen to enter the roommate experience open to learning and compromise and to stand up for his needs. Being honest and clear will usually be the best way to proceed in most roommate relationships.

Sharing Expenses

Even in a small dorm room there may be a need for a few shared expenses. Working this out tends to be roommate challenge number one. It provides a great opening for negotiation and working out differences in values. For example, if one roommate has more money and wants to share the cost of an expensive sound system that isn't important or feasible for the other roommate, the uninterested party must be honest about that. Expectations and assumptions are what get tricky. The more clearly these differences in wants and needs are voiced, the better understood any solution will be.

Health Care Details

Before your teen leaves home, make sure he has an annual physical exam with his doctor, a dental checkup and teeth-cleaning appointment with the dentist, and an eye exam. If other appointments with specialists are part of your teen's regular health care, set them up early in the summer before life becomes rushed. These appointments also provide a good vehicle for conversation and cooperation, and offer an opportunity to begin shifting the responsibility for personal health to your teen. Be sure to provide your child with a copy of his medical and dental cards, the contact information for his physicians, and any medical records and copies he should have when he moves out.

Freshman Orientation

If your teen is headed to college, orientation is your student's ticket to the information she will need and use every day throughout the year, so don't miss it. At many colleges, freshman orientation is set up for both student and parents. If distance makes it unaffordable for both of you to attend, send your student and ask her to collect double copies of all paperwork so you'll have a set of your own. If at all possible, go in person with your teen. It's an excellent chance for the two of you to absorb the campus "feel" and to learn how it works. The excitement of change ahead is in the air at freshman orientation. It's also a great way to learn many of the details of the campus life your teen is about to embrace.

You may feel overwhelmed (even sobered) by some of the information you receive at the new-student orientation. But eventually everything will all make sense. I still refer to a brochure I received at orientation that gives details of payment schedules, the academic calendar, financial aid contacts, housing choices, health insurance options, available meal programs, and ways to pay for food, laundry, and more. It has been invaluable. Most of this information is available online on college and university Web sites. But time and again, I have dug up this brochure and found the single piece of information and phone number I needed. Alert your teen that she will probably receive financial communications from the school (both e-mail and written) that she should discuss and pass along to you.

Freshman orientation will apprise you of more new dates to place on the family calendar—dates that your teen should also put on his: due dates for acceptance deposits, first-term tuition, meal plans, and room and board. If periodic or delayed payment plans are available, you'll have to factor those into the calendar. You'll also have to determine how financial aid will affect payment deadlines. Another crucial date is your teen's course selection deadline for first-year registration.

At orientation, you and your teen can find out (if you don't know already) how to determine the amount of credit the college or university will give for Advanced Placement (AP), College Level Examination Program (CLEP), or International Baccalaureate (IB) exams and classes. Your teen should ask her school counselor to forward that information to the college registrar in order to receive credit. This is well worth the extra effort and can save you wads of tuition money. Some students are able to register with advanced standing as second-term freshmen or even as sophomores, which will give them greater accessibility to classes of specific interest.

Instead of reviewing college guides as in past summers, you'll find your teen poring over a course catalog, trying to figure out which courses are available to him. He may look at required courses, classes available in his major course of study (if known), and subjects in areas of study that are new and simply intriguing.

Read the catalogs together to locate guidelines for semester credit loads and criteria for full- and part-time student status. This will differ from school to school. If your teen is also participating in a time-consuming sport or art form that requires long hours of practice, it is probably smartest to start at the low end, rather than the high end, of required course credits. In general, a full-time load of courses will help guarantee that your child will graduate in four years. A full-time load often means best financial aid and health insurance benefits for parents as well. However, many students do take a less-than-full-time course load, depending on their situation. For example, a student with special health considerations may need a less demanding schedule in order to accommodate particular limitations.

Managing Time

College work requires a huge adjustment. Some teens naively expect they can do it all—school, work, extracurriculars, social life—as easily as when they were in high school. But, on the whole, college is more rigorous and demanding, and teens must figure out for themselves how to concentrate effectively, meet deadlines, and handle the increased expectations for academic achievement.

Talk with your teen about time management. So much of college success is about learning to balance time and the demands of academics and life. You probably already have a sense of your child's skill in this area, but it never hurts to talk about the importance of prioritizing competing demands and using time well. In a new environment, with so much action all around them and so many distractions, most teens learn that conscious effort is required to concentrate and manage time well, even for the most conscientious students. This is something to keep in mind as your teen chooses his courses and schedules.

Reinventing the Rules

No doubt as the time approaches to leave home, teens may have "left" already, especially when it comes to curfew and other rules. Some parents admit that once their son or daughter graduates, they would be willing to bend an evening curfew in ways they might not have done before. But, at the same time, it is more than acceptable to ask them to balance their late night arrivals with your own need to sleep and awaken refreshed for work the next day.

Cell phones and text messaging create ideal avenues for direct communication. Even without a cell phone, your teen can remain responsible about staying in touch. Devise creative ways to connect with your teen without being too invasive—leaving notes works well, too. At this point in family life, your teen ideally should understand the need for mutual respect that is necessary to live successfully with others (including you and future roommates), and you should ideally recognize your teen's need for greater freedom of movement and decision-making as he is on the verge of leaving home.

Now is the time to begin the shift from hands-on parenting to a more hands-off style. This is also the moment for respectful discussion and consensus building, rather than for control, discipline, and hovering. Our time as parents who actively implement discipline and teach new behaviors is coming to an end. It is, however, the beginning for many parents in forging a new way to be with kids.

During the summer before your son or daughter leaves home, begin an ongoing conversation about the changes and challenges to the parent/child relationship that lie ahead. Although you've probably expressed your values about drinking, relationships, sexuality, academic goals, and spirituality in the past, and these values are, to a certain extent, already in place within your teen, these same values will continue to be shaped by your teen's experiences living independently of you. As parents, we cannot help but feel this summer offers a final chance to impart wise words.

Experimenting with Alcohol

Excessive drinking is one of the biggest issues facing teens in the years they're learning to live independently. The seeds of our values around drinking, and its associations with sexual situations and other drug use, have already long been planted in our children, but it's still valuable to talk about them *again*. Everything changes when a teen moves from home base to a completely peer-centered existence. It's a hot zone for peer influence. High school was fraught with this sort of influence, but when parental boundaries are removed, teens encounter a huge new playing field of opportunity. They really will have to figure out things in this area for themselves.

Colleges, even those that declare "dry campuses," struggle with the drinking issue. There is little doubt that every student will have to make choices about his own relationship with alcohol and other drugs in a setting where they will be constantly available and where alcohol abuse often becomes normalized.

What's the genetic makeup of your family? Do you need to revisit or remind your teen of a family predisposition toward alcoholism or addiction? When teens first begin to live independently, without parental supervision and boundaries, the time is ripe for experimentation. Even if only to heighten the awareness of what lies ahead for your teen, be certain to raise this issue. Better for your child to be grumpy with you and enter college with a more acute awareness of the consequences than to be totally caught off guard.

Making Decisions about Sexual Behavior

Author Harlan Cohen writes in *The Naked Roommate: And 107 Other Issues You Might Run Into in College* that "college is *the place*" to contract a sexually transmitted disease or infection. He says, "The challenge—you don't always know who has them and who doesn't. One in five college-age people has at least one." Everything happens fast in college. Students were far less concerned about STDs in years past. In fact, many of us were oblivious to the hazards of HIV/AIDS, which only became a public health issue beginning in the mid–1980s. No one can now afford that kind of near-sightedness. The risks are far too great.

Aside from moral and ethical considerations, teens need to hear (again and again) from parents that unprotected sex can result in lifelong consequences. While each student makes an individual decision about whether and when to become sexually active, it is a serious decision, and one closely connected to the family and religious values we transmit to our children and teens. Although abstinence can be lonely and difficult, it resolves all the worries about sexual health: about pregnancy, overemotional involve-ment too early in a relationship, the possibility of contract-ing STDs, and so on.

Although we all hope our children will avoid risky situa-tions, some sexual behavior and exploration is the norm for most college students. Fortunately, a wide range of birth control options exist. This is an area in which it's important for parents to think ahead and prepare teens well, above all nurturing in them the virtues of thoughtfulness, advance planning, knowing their core values, and taking responsibil-ity for their choices.

As young adults, teens are about to enter a new pressure zone. Instead of returning home to sleep, they are on their own, 24 hours a day, and will no doubt spend time taking full advantage of newfound liberties. Do what you can to encour-age your teen to be clear about her values and be ready to hold true to those values, even when she is surrounded by multiple, competing value systems. Part of the beauty of this stage is the way the world is expanding for your teen—so many different kinds of people to meet, so many topics to study, encounter, and learn from. The stronger your teen's own core values, the less likely she will be to bend herself to fit in with others' needs or feel the need to judge those who live their lives differently from how she lives hers.

Relationship Highs, Lows, and In-Betweens

The road to love is often winding and rocky, especially for this age group. If it hasn't happened already, we will, at some point, experience vicariously through our teenage children various encounters with one or more of the following: rejec-tion, heartache, confusion, difficulty ending a bad relation-ship, hanging on for the wrong reasons, the euphoria of crazy love followed by first-fight trauma, and loneliness.

As parents, we can listen and advise when we are asked. But we are also limited in this arena. These are our children's hearts—and they will be warmed, lightened, scarred, and healed, just like our own have been.

Of course, every cellular impulse we experience as parents is driven to save our children from any pain. Except for locking them in a box and throwing away the key, however, there is no sparing a young person from heartache. Hearts learn love by loving both wisely and foolishly. Teens deserve their own learning curve.

One source of strength that many teens can draw upon to buffer themselves against relationship highs and lows is their close friends, both male and female. Friendship is the great training ground for intimacy. Whatever ups and downs your teen experiences in the world of love, his healthy friendships will help him right himself and teach him what he wants and needs in a mature relationship.

Moving beyond the Hometown Sweetheart

Mary's daughter, Caroline, left for college vowing to maintain her relationship with her high school boyfriend. Although Caroline and her boyfriend made a good team and Mary was fond of him, she wished they had made a clean break, agreeing to start college unencumbered. In several conversations with her daughter, Mary gently pointed out why Caroline might feel limited by hanging on to a hometown boyfriend.

During Caroline's first semester away, Mary felt that Caroline's boyfriend provided her daughter with a sense of security. For Caroline, highlights of the semester were visits from him and to his campus. Mary wondered how much time the two spent texting, e-mailing, and talking instead of trying out new activities and getting to know new people. But she could also see how the relationship in some ways soothed her daughter's transition into college life.

Caroline's boyfriend initiated the breakup, right before final exams, making a focus on finals difficult for Caroline. Mary comforted and supported her daughter as best she could by phone and e-mail, but felt in the long run that the breakup was a good thing. Caroline's roommate was helpful, and she also received support from a new study group friend. This friend had also experienced a recent breakup, and she and Caroline met regularly for coffee and study time, helping each other through the heartbreak period. By the time her spring semester ended, Caroline had cried, gotten angry, and moved on, ready to return the next fall and become more involved in her school. She joined an intramural soccer team and was excited about her new classes. Even she could see that the breakup freed her to try new activities that she hadn't made time for earlier.

In the end, teens sometimes wish they had moved out unencumbered by high school romantic relationships. But they may also benefit from the regular conversation and long-distance support, a comfort during all the adjusting that goes on in the first months after leaving home. Parents may wish they could save their teens from the heartache of ending a long-term relationship, but the reality is that parent support is what is most meaningful, done in the best way you know how. You can discuss the difficulty of maintaining a long-distance relationship with your teen, but ultimately, your child may need to experience it for herself.

DETAILS, CONVERSATIONS, AND DECISIONS

➤ Renegotiate family rules where it makes sense during these last months of living together, but hold firm on what you need.

➤ Allow packing and preparing to be a time to help and guide your child and to enjoy his or her company and excitement about what lies ahead.

➤ Read all forms from your student's school or program carefully. Underline responsibilities and deadlines that you need to take care of, and be sure your teen knows his responsibilities and deadlines, too. Share those details with your teen.

➤ Mark the calendar with payment due dates for items such as deposits, room and board fees, tuition, meal plan charges, and student activity fees.

➤ Follow through with all financial and registration paperwork, keeping a notebook or folder of receipts, school mailings, and newsletters. Let your student know about your progress.

➤ Mark deadlines for course registration on your calendar and be sure your teen notes the date. Often, the sooner a student registers, the greater the chance she has of getting into the courses she wants.

➤ Note the due dates for residence hall preferences and roommate questionnaires. Encourage your teen to fill you in on his progress.

➤ Agree upon a way and a time to communicate regularly when your teen moves out: IM? Phone? E-mail? Snail mail? Or a combination!

➤ Have those difficult but necessary conversations with your teen about alcohol and drug use, sexual behavior, and values. Listen carefully, and speak respectfully. If your teen is, or may become, sexually active, make sure he or she has access to birth control and protection.

CHAPTER 8

Living at Home after Graduation

For some teens, living at home while they are attending college or vocational-technical school, or while they are working and performing community service, may be the "just right" decision. In difficult economic times, living at home longer makes sense for more and more teens and their families. Given the contracting job market, the declining sources of financial aid, and the high cost of living, opportunities for true economic and social independence are harder to come by. Living at home while taking classes and/or working can be an effective way to prepare for the next move.

Choosing to live at home longer may also be tied to a teen's emotional needs or the realization that he or she does not yet have the maturity to move out and live independently. Developmental maturation depends on complex biological and environmental factors. In addition, loss or trauma can also affect a teen's readiness to leave home. In so many ways, it is better for a family to be realistic and face the possibility that a teen is not quite ready to move out, rather than pushing their child into a premature move and spending time and energy later picking up the pieces. Many successful adults have taken this route through their late teens.

For the parent of a teen who needs and chooses to live longer at home, your role is a complex one to sort through. As one father of an 18-year-old boy remarked, "Some kids need a longer incubation period than others. It's just a more delicate [process] to figure out my role as dad to this almost-adult child when he is in the kitchen every day—often making a mess." A number of parents struggle with the feeling that they have somehow failed as a parent because their teens weren't ready to leave home. Teens also may initially feel self-conscious about choosing to remain at home. Sometimes, one of the most important things you can do as a parent is accept that living at home may be just what your child needs.

➤ ——————————————————————————————

When a Learning Disability Complicates the Launch

Brigid's daughter needed extra academic help throughout her school years. A learning disability had made studying and testing especially difficult, and she worked hard just to keep up. For several reasons, Brigid's daughter wasn't ready to move away from home for college. Toward the end of her daughter's junior year, Brigid discovered a citywide collaborative of community and technical colleges and thought the program might be perfect for her daughter. It provided two years of tuition-free study, individualized academic advising, career development services, peer support programs, and social and cultural activities. Brigid brought home information about the program, arranged an appointment with a school counselor to learn more, and helped her daughter apply. Program advisers felt her daughter was a good match, and she enrolled.

Brigid also encouraged her daughter to find a job. Applying and interviewing pushed this young woman out of her comfort zone—in a positive way. The security her daughter felt from continuing to live at home allowed her to branch out gradually, take college classes, and work, growing and maturing as she did so—without the added pressure of adapting to a new living situation.

In the fall, Brigid found herself doing the delicate parental dance of expressing both empathy and tough love for her daughter when she experienced a rough period after her best friends left for college. Fall is an emotionally difficult time for any teen who stays behind. Extra understanding, encouragement, and compassion are required from parents to help ease the passage. This young woman learned to reach out to old friends who were still in town, as well as engage with new friends she met at school and work. Brigid worked hard to give her the space to test the consequences of her decisions. Living at home after graduation proved to be a good decision.

Setting Your Limits

Living with your young adult while she or he pursues work, school, or additional training requires extra effort from parents. Patience, certainly, but also an ongoing effort to assess your parenting: too much? too little? Be clear about your own limits on what is acceptable and unacceptable. The end goal is to help your teen move toward financial, intellectual, and emotional independence, supporting her responsible decisions even when it might be difficult to watch her deal with the consequences of her decisions. Be clear about your expectations and family boundaries. Seek outside help when necessary and keep a positive vision of your teen's independence before you.

As with many challenges in life, it is helpful for teens and parents to know they are not alone. Living at home after graduation simply makes good financial and developmental sense for many teens (and twentysomethings too). Encourage your teen to connect with others in the same boat, and do the same as a parent. Realize that you are part of a much larger group to make this particular family decision, and be confident that it can be a positive and productive experience for you, your teen, and your entire family.

GUIDELINES FOR LAUNCHING FROM HOME BASE

➤ Seek out people you trust who have shared their home with their high school graduates. Ask what works for them and what doesn't. Did they share expenses? Split household chores? Rotate the family car? Ask for their best advice.

➤ Research post–high school options and encourage your teen to do the same by talking to her school counselor. Seek out work and school programs available to teens through the community and technical school system in your area. Use the Internet to pinpoint possibilities, and make an appointment to talk to an admissions counselor. Attend the appointment with your teen, if it's appropriate.

➤ Give yourself time to embark on a trial-and-error period of learning what it's like to be the parent of an out-of-high-school young adult.

➤ Decide what boundaries and expectations you will set with your teen, and clearly communicate them. What should quiet hours be? Who is responsible for housework (and child care, in some cases)? What financial contribution should each of you make toward the family's expenses? How will you all care for common space in the kitchen, bathroom, and family areas?

➤ Make a conscious effort to treat your young adult as a roommate rather than as a dependent. Treat your teen with respect, and support his attempts to stretch himself in new ways.

➤ Remember that your teen can live at home, be productive, and still constructively ready herself for independent living. Let your choices and attitudes as a parent reflect this ultimate goal.

CHAPTER 9

Independent Living
(and All That Comes with It)

Whether your teen moves solo into a residence hall, shares a room with one or more roommates, or ends up in communal housing with five to a room or suite, the independent-living curve will be both gradual *and* steep. The more flexible your son or daughter, the better. Let your child know ahead of time that much will be new—and new requires adaptation and the passage of time to feel at home in a different and unfamiliar environment. "The truth is that you might not find your place right away when you start college. It takes work and time," says Harlan Cohen, author of *The Naked Roommate: And 107 Other Issues You Might Run Into in College.*

Living Alone

Occasionally, students may have the option of rooming alone when they move out of the home. Issues with roommates will not directly affect them. However, even with a room of their own, most teens still negotiate some kind of shared living space, whether it's the use of a common bathroom, or kitchen, or living room, so the issues of living with others will ultimately affect them in some way.

And although teens living alone have more control over their own small living space, solo living can also present particular challenges. It requires more effort to connect with others through various ways. There will be no automatic connection to someone else's plans or friends or group energy. To encourage the kind of spontaneous "drop by" connections that come more easily when one is living with a roommate, the single dweller in a secure dormitory can leave his door open at times. The single dweller also must learn to leave his room and get involved in classes and other activities to meet people and make friends. A natural starting point for building relationships can be the one person he knows or an activity he is especially enthusiastic about.

Colleges abound with groups, activities, and clubs that are open to everyone. They include groups for energetic athletes, musicians of all types, devoted chess players, political fans of every stripe, religious organizations, computer gamers, and more. You name it, and your teen may well be able to find other like-minded souls participating in an activity that has appeal. If your teen ends up in a single room, encourage her to open the door, step outside, and join in campus life.

Freshmen Roommates

Many freshmen-to-be make contact with their future roommates over the summer. Since roommate assignments are usually made by the school, it's helpful to stress to your teen that living with someone you don't know can be a valuable learning experience and a lesson in getting along with people who may not share your background and values. It is helpful for parents to realize that it will be just as powerful an experience for your teen to share a room with someone new as it will be for him to study new subjects and learn his way around an unfamiliar place.

Getting Used to Different Lifestyles

This category contains a huge range of possible learning experiences for your child. Above all, it's important to realize what an incredible mind- and heart-opener college and community programs can be. Your teen has the opportunity to learn about and see up close all the endless variations in the way people live their lives, from ways of dressing and eating to styles of worship and political preferences to conduct in personal relationships. Sharing a living space (most often initially with complete strangers) is a huge part of the cultural learning experience for this age group.

In the beginning, you'll probably receive a few phone calls from your teen venting about the downside of this shared life. Sympathy is always a good thing to offer, but encourage your child to be open to learning from others while taking care of her own needs. Most kids go off to school wanting a positive living experience, and in most cases it's possible—especially if your teen and her roommates talk, negotiate, and set up rules they all agree upon and adhere to. The sooner the rules are set, the better. And the sooner issues of conflict are aired, the better. The more difficult cases are often those where unspoken feelings and opinions build to a point of resentment and cause a blowup.

Setting personal limits can be key for your teen. Limits range from how much money she can spend to when she needs quiet time to study or sleep. The frequency of overnight guests is an issue that has to be worked out, especially if one or both roommates has a steady boyfriend or girlfriend. It is most effective to work things out openly—so as parents, hopefully we have trained our kids in the art of effective communication and can keep encouraging them to use it.

As a college freshman, my teen rowed many mornings at 5:00 a.m. She learned to be very quiet on those mornings, using a flashlight to dress in the dark. In return, her roommate was similarly quiet or left their room during the evenings when my teen needed to turn in early. The two worked out a respectful relationship even though they kept different schedules. They didn't necessarily have an easy time sharing a room, but they did forge a mutual respect for each other, sometimes through difficult conversations and at times through periods of not speaking.

In that first year, excitement over having a new roommate gave way to irritation, followed by a period of barely speaking to each other, and finally to hard-won, respectful coexistence. In other words, the two roommates learned from each other how to live together peacefully. I have always appreciated my teen's roommate for the emotional maturity she displayed and the ability she displayed in respecting another's choices, even if they were different from her own. Better yet, my daughter appreciated her roommate's considerateness, too. Mutual respect was the key goal here, but every roommate story will differ.

Caring for Personal Health

Sleep deprivation is an important personal health concern for this age group. Surrounded by so many fun and interesting people, with so much going on! As a parent, you may have little direct control in this area, but you can gently remind your child of the benefits of adequate sleep, especially as a preventative for illness. Because it isn't fun for teens to be sick, prevention might be something they care about. When students do fall ill, they need to seek out the campus health center or a nearby clinic in a timely manner to get the medical care they need.

Most colleges offer students affordable health insurance. Information usually is sent with admission and enrollment information. Look into this option, but factor in any existing family health insurance policies and the provisions they make for family members under age 23. Many parents have health coverage that includes college-age students as long as they are enrolled in school at least half time. Check with your health insurance company to confirm your current coverage and to learn whether your child will need additional health insurance.

Shared bathrooms and community spaces are what one nurse calls "petri dish" settings. In other words, these areas are conducive to germ growth. It's a good idea for teens to wear flip-flops on shared bathroom and kitchen floors, and it's a basic health promotion measure for them to avoid sharing cups and utensils. A good daily multivitamin can provide additional health benefits, and it never hurts to remind your teen of the importance of nutritious food, regular exercise, and adequate sleep (just in case she or he is listening).

Developing Safety Awareness

Personal safety is a big issue on college campuses, and most campus administrations are keenly aware of this. Many schools provide security escort services at night, and schools may place emergency phones in key locations, along with lighting every 50 feet or so. When students live off campus, it is important that they let someone know where they are and make arrangements to head home from a late night of studying or socializing accompanied by a friend or other trusted person, at the very least letting a roommate know when they are on their way home.

"Date rape" is, unfortunately, not uncommon among

18- to 22-year-olds. Fueled by alcohol and other substances, social situations can quickly escalate out of control. Remaining sober and alert, and communicating intentions clearly can forestall some negative interactions, but fighting back with the help of pepper spray can also be helpful. Young men and women need the communication skills that enable them to set personal boundaries and face situations that progress from harmless to invasive, even possibly violent. Armed with accurate information, personal awareness, and good friends, many teens can avoid such an experience. Because drinking may cloud judgment and weaken the ability to think clearly and act decisively, alcohol is often cited as a factor in date rape (along with substances such as Rohypnol, which is tasteless, colorless, and easily slipped into drinks). For more information about date rape drugs, see www.womenshealth.gov/faq. Talk to your teen about these issues and keep the lines of communication open.

One study of sexual predators concludes that they tend to prey on women who are talking on cell phones, digging in purses or bags, wearing headphones, or are otherwise distracted. Fighting back, yelling, using mace or pepper spray, or even shouting that you have spray can scare an attacker away. Remind your teen that predators are often looking for easy targets. While this kind of victimization is relatively uncommon, it is important that your student understand how to protect herself from it.

Nurturing Friendships

"A lot of people leave for college thinking they will make new friends immediately, and they panic if they don't . . . but the real problem is thinking that it all should happen so fast. It's not normal. Friendships take a long time to form," writes Harlan Cohen in his insightful book *The Naked Roommate:*

And 107 Other Issues You Might Run Into in College. So often your teen's high school friends have been his friends for years. Chances are you know the parents and may count those parents as your own friends. But college friendships are a whole new experience for teens. Remind your child that it may take time to form new friendships. Finding friends when a teen first arrives on campus seems daunting for many. This is where a teen's involvement in clubs, special interest groups, and campus activities (other than partying) can be very helpful.

Activity groups that meet and bond over time provide a built-in group of potential friends. Intramural sports teams often work, as do choral and theater groups, which give many students a way to make both male and female friends. Our daughter's sports teammates shared numerous highs and lows together during their freshman year. She emerged from the experience counting her teammates among her closest college friends. Without the team experience, she might have had a more difficult time finding friends. In her junior year, she joined a group that planned campus activities and developed several more important friendships.

Friendship requires time and patience, commodities that teens are not necessarily known for. You may need to gently remind your teen of the effort it takes to be receptive to new friendships and that the timing and magic of friendships is not something that can be rushed or forced.

CONVERSATIONS ABOUT INDEPENDENT LIVING

➤ Talk to your teen about the realities of living with a roommate and stress the value of communicating clearly and responsibly to keep conflicts at a minimum.

➤ Encourage your teen to have an open mind toward new roommates and learning experiences. Both parents and teens will find value in Harlan Cohen's book *The Naked Roommate: And 107 Other Issues You Might Run Into in College*, which is filled with practical information on these topics and many others.

➤ Talk to your teen about personal care: get adequate sleep, visit the campus or local clinic for prompt medical care for health concerns, carry a health insurance card, eat vitamin-rich foods, find time to exercise, talk about reasonable boundaries with roommates, and keep an open mind when it comes to differences.

➤ Review personal safety issues with your teen and encourage her or him to call a campus security escort or join up with a friend when walking after dark.

➤ Talk to your teen about nurturing new friendships and taking time to reach out to others through class, group, and team activities.

➤ Remind your son or daughter that this is an exciting time of life. Not *every* moment will be exciting, but many, many good times lie ahead.

CHAPTER 10

Pack, Unload, and Leave

The time finally came to leave her at college. We hugged and kissed good-bye. As we drove away, she bounded up the steps of Oak Ridge Hall. She didn't look back.

DANA ESSEX, *"BUT I'M NOT READY YET"*

T he sheets have been purchased and your teen has contacted the new roommate to negotiate (and try to prevent bringing dual) items that have to fit into a small space. Lists made by you and/or your teen are being closely scrutinized and, hopefully, items are being checked off. Packing is exciting and nostalgic at the same time. You may notice (but try not to dwell on) the fact that every time you peer inside, your teen's room looks a bit more empty.

How much space is going to be available to your teen in his new living quarters is a big factor in deciding what and what not to pack. As a parent, you want to emphasize this and encourage him to leave some things behind. When school is a four-hour drive away, you may be able to make a deal on objects your teen is undecided about packing: to leave something home initially, and if he decides he has both the space and the need for it, you can bring it on a future visit.

When college is farther away and flight is your mode of transportation, your child's packing is automatically limited. Sometimes parents take advantage of an airline's maximum bag limits and pack as much as possible per person.

Others ship easily packed items like towels and clothes. Rather than ship many boxes, though, or drive a car full of items a long distance, it can be far more economical and just plain easier to buy a used desk or coffeemaker near campus and get it to school in a rental car.

Deliver, Drop Off, and Say Good-bye

The day we first drove our daughter to college remains emblazoned in memory. It was beautiful and sunny, and the process of moving her into the dorm was well organized. The four of us—myself, my daughter, my husband, and our younger son—pulled in at the scheduled time, received a two-hour temporary parking sticker, and began to unload. Once we were in her room, we checked the dorm layout, met her roommate, and grabbed an enormous cart to begin the loading and hauling process. Our son, sad to be losing his day-to-day life with his much-admired older sister, stuck close to her, and we all focused on the task at hand. All around us, moms and dads and siblings and favorite aunts and uncles were all doing the same thing. The air was filled with an electric current, emotionally charged and alive.

That day of delivery and drop-off is intense for parents and teens—and there's no way around it. Besides the palpable emotion, a swell of excitement and energy fills the air. Nobody can beat college-age kids for fun and energy. Our daughter's university had sent an abundance of material for freshmen and their parents, including an injunction to remain upbeat on moving day but *not* to linger too long. So that's what we did. We shook hands with her roommate, helped her unload and set up, and then hugged and kissed and bade her good-bye. In the interests of remaining upbeat, my husband and I teared up slightly, but we didn't let out our intense emotions. I had wondered if I would cry all the way home, but found myself more in a state of quiet shock.

We drove home in a suspended state. There was something about that drive. It was hard to know what to say. The biggest news was that we had just dropped off our daughter/sister; she would no longer ever really live with us again, except for short stints. Life was in the process of shifting for all of us. We were all a little bit sad and probably a little envious of her, too (especially her younger brother). Clearly, she had embarked on a new adventure that did not include us.

And the three of us? We were returning to our regular lives, this time without her energy and daily presence. Each rotation of the wheels brought us closer to home and farther from her new life. What would our new life without her be like? As with so many losses, there is no way to really prepare for the magnitude of this day. So the three of us got back in our car, turned up the radio, sang along once in a while, and watched the green hills roll by.

It's a huge moment—you realize that you have always been preparing your child for this day, steadily encouraging independence and skill-building, step-by-step. Now, here you are, launching your child in his own boat. It is time for him to set sail and navigate unknown waters, sending him off on his own exciting journey in the face of unpredictable winds and weather.

How will our children do? Have we taught them enough? The answer is in the adventure of their lives. As in our own, there will be ups and downs, moments of feeling lost, but also times of steadily building confidence that hopefully leads toward a successful adulthood. The day of drop-off is the momentous beginning of this passage.

The Sweetness and Sorrow of Good-bye

On the day before Maureen's husband flew across the country with their oldest son to settle him in to his new college, her college-bound son spent a final day with his younger brothers and his mother. They went out for lunch and spent time together at the beach. She was struck by the amount of time they spent quietly, just being together. Talking about the change ahead didn't seem right to any of them, and so her memory is a peaceful one of a pleasant last day together with all the children right before the moment of change. Later that evening, after helping her son with last-minute packing, she slipped into her room as emotion washed over her. The time had come to say, "You've been a great kid to raise." How did it come so fast?

A New Life Begins

Mitch chose a small school on the West Coast. Since his family lived in the Midwest, it was clear to his parents that flying made more sense than taking a week off work to drive both ways. Mitch's parents decided to leave their younger daughter with a friend so that both of them could go, and they each brought two bags that Mitch packed full of his things.

When the three arrived, they rented a car. Heather and her husband stayed for a couple of days to help him set up his dorm room and shop for the small things they hadn't had room to pack. It was a special time for them all, those brief final days of face-to-face conversation, with no competition from his younger sister.

Mitch's school specified a time for parents to leave. When that time came and Mitch asked his parents, "Now what do I do?" Heather felt her heart break a bit. It was hard to say good-bye because Mitch had a single room and no roommate. Heather showed him the college calendar of events, pointed out the freshman picnic that was just starting, and said, "Just walk up the hill—you'll find a whole bunch of freshman like yourself who are not quite sure what to do next."

Months later, the moment stays with her—that moment of letting go. The time had come for her son to figure out what to do next without them. Leaving was not easy, but both parties survived. Mitch did go to the picnic and found a person he already knew. He met new people, too. This was the beginning of his new life.

Role Reversal

Celia and her daughter traveled, just the two of them, to her daughter's new college town, arriving a few days early and staying in a nearby hotel. Celia could sense her daughter readying herself as she packed and repacked. Mother and daughter made a couple of trips to buy linens and other items they hadn't brought with them. They loaded it all into a couple of large suitcases they'd brought along.

Celia had called a neighbor whose daughter attended the same university and asked for advice about getting around without a car and finding the kinds of supplies that college girls typically need. By the time moving day had arrived, both Celia and her daughter were fairly comfortable navigating the city, especially the area near the university.

Celia hailed a cab, hauling the big suitcases along. During the ride, the cab driver, a man recently emigrated from Africa, said to her daughter, "Your parents are giving you a real gift. You are so fortunate, and it is so important that you make the most of it." Celia said she had tears in her eyes. It was exactly the way she herself felt, and here, a complete stranger was saying it for her with heartfelt passion. It was as if the voice of the universe had found a way to personally deliver a message to her daughter.

After helping her daughter unload and unpack, Celia noticed a dorm sign advertising the first hall meeting, followed by dinner. She and her daughter looked at each other and Celia told her, "I think you should go do that. I'll be at the hotel if you need me, but otherwise I think it's time to say good-bye." Since Celia was taking home the empty suitcases and it was raining outside, her daughter replied, "You shouldn't walk in this weather. I'll catch a cab for you."

Already her daughter was taking charge, caring for her mother in the way her mother had been caring for her. Celia was aware of the shift in responsibility from one adult to another. She cherished her daughter for looking out for her needs. After hugs and good-byes, Celia took the cab back to her hotel and caught an early-morning flight home.

So much preparation goes into the decision about what to do after high school that when it comes right down to the time a child actually embarks in a new direction, it is overlaid with all sorts of emotion, for both parents and the teen. And there is an actual moment of departure and transition between what was and what will be. It's a moment tinged with some loss and anxiety, so be gentle with yourself. But it is also a moment to be celebrated, truly a crossing over.

FINAL TO-DO LIST

➤ Pack up—your teen should make the list and check it twice, but you can check it, too!

➤ Have a personal computer on hand for your teen—it is a must. Check out the college's specific hardware and software recommendations.

➤ Ship the light stuff by mail if your teen is moving a considerable distance.

➤ Ask your teen what items can wait. Sometimes what seems to be a necessity back home can fade in importance in the reality of a small space.

➤ Gather yourself together for the good-bye. (Talk to others who have done this. If your best source of support isn't there with you, have your phone handy.)

➤ Hard as it may be, do leave when they (the college authorities that be) suggest you go. There has yet to be a college student who didn't survive a parent's good-bye.

CHAPTER 11

This Is It! The Parenting Shift

A college administrator's advice to incoming freshman parents: "Be busy yourself. Too much time to worry won't be good for your child or you." After Suzanne dropped her son off at college, she came home feeling happy. He was in a place that he was excited about. He had been difficult to live with in many ways his last few months at home. Suzanne knew his new setting was good for him and made him happy. So a couple of weeks later she was surprised by the way his absence began to sink in and hit her hard. He was gone—most likely never to live at home again. She described her feelings that day:

> *It's an elemental loss. So deep it's almost instinctual. And it has nothing to do with whether or not I have—or other parents have—a strong enough life of my own. It's separate from that. I still have a child at home. But this son is gone; and gone is the part of me that parented him on a day-to-day basis. People don't talk about it much, but it's like having a boulder of grief inside me.*

Feeling the Shift

A child's departure represents a change in the life of the family. It's one of those milestones that carries a bitter-sweet edge to it. Of course, you are happy that your child is able and willing to venture into the adult world. But all the time and energy that went into raising that child is now replaced temporarily by an empty, open space. Sure, there will be phone calls and visits, but things will never be quite the same.

A father who has successfully launched three children says it was hardest to say good-bye to the first. That's when the family realizes it is profoundly shifting. Eighteen years of living together as parents, child, and younger siblings is now over. And when just one child remains at home, the whole family shifts and feels different. One mother commented, "In the past with both kids, we would mount an expedition for an activity or for dinner, but now it feels harder. Those first meals without the oldest were almost awkward. I can see that it's hard on our daughter to suddenly be an only child."

A Father's Sadness

One father, Jeff, expected his wife to feel sad in the weeks after they took their son to college, but he wasn't prepared for the effect it had on him. His wife had always worked part time and been available for their son's typical teen activities. Jeff worked long hours and frequently traveled, yet he always made an effort to be involved in his son's activities, went to baseball games with him, and enjoyed hanging out at home with him.

Because work had been his life's primary focus, Jeff was shocked at how the empty house reverberated with the echo of his son's absence and surprised by how much he missed the easy camaraderie the two had shared, especially when the sports report was broadcast on the evening news. The first few weeks were infused with a longing that nearly took his breath away. Sometimes Jeff wandered into his son's room in the evening; that always made him nostalgic for his son.

Moving On

Heather couldn't believe how quickly the moment arrived to say good-bye to her son, Mitch. For a couple of days, the intensity of his departure washed over her. "In a way it was like experiencing a mini-death." Heather spoke of how a physical space opened up in the home, along with a new feeling. She says, "At first the psychological space felt like pure emptiness. I wasn't at all sure what to do with it. And I spent the first couple of weeks feeling lost, sometimes wandering into his room, worrying about how my quiet son was doing in the middle of all those people. Then it occurred to me that I could do something with that space—read a book, go for a long bike ride. I began to see that the disorienting loss could find its way into new freedom."

Forging New Communication Patterns

In her essay "But I'm Not Ready Yet," Dana Essex writes, "Parents' Weekend came and went—[our daughter] didn't look back then, either. She's been home to see friends and stop in briefly. She calls, she texts, and she 'pokes' me and her dad on Facebook. She even asked me to call her more often a couple of weekends ago. I'm not looking back so much now. And it's not as hard as I was sure it would be."

Another mother, Heather, discovered the parent-sharing Web site for her son's college to be a great resource. She didn't feel so alone with her worries or struggle so much with her son's infrequent communication. Heather learned that infrequent contact is how newly independent teens separate and develop their own identity. If lack of communication made her feel lonely for Mitch, she could remind herself that this was part of his becoming his own person.

Our daughter called often during her first year away—

almost daily, and usually between classes. I pictured her walking across campus, phone to her ear. Conversations were usually short but had the effect of a running conversation. I knew there would be more of those conversations when she came home at the holidays, and other built-in opportunities for visits would crop up. I learned early on to let our daughter initiate most of the contacts. It just seemed to work better that way. Occasionally I would place a call, but for the most part conversation flowed better when she called, at a time and from a place that was good for her.

Although e-mail is frequently a primary form of correspondence, nothing replaces the gift of a handwritten note, or a typed note bearing a handwritten signature. Care packages are another great way to connect with your college student, especially at final exam time. Students love these. If your student is a passionate coffee or smoothie drinker (so many are), he may appreciate an occasional gift card to his favorite chain, along with a note, or perhaps some vitamins or a pair of socks with a favorite magazine thrown in. Our daughter always seemed to appreciate these gestures.

Visits from Your Teen

Your teen's visits home are often highlights of that first year—for students and for parents. The most common visits occur around Thanksgiving, the winter holidays, and spring break, although these breaks are sometimes limited by distance and finances. Students living closer to home may return more often, especially freshmen. Usually they come home to rejuvenate. College life—and the changes that go with it—is demanding. Expect your new relationship with your emerging adult child to be forged in fits and starts.

As wonderful as these visits are, they can also be disorienting for both teens and parents. By November, your freshman has become fully immersed in a new life—one that you do not share and that she cannot fully convey. In fact, it can be a challenge to relate it to her old friends, too. Where do the new parts of herself fit in back home? How constrained will her newly independent self feel by the familiar family roof?

One father described a party his son planned for his high school friends over the Thanksgiving break. They gathered at the house the night after Thanksgiving and exchanged stories all night long. This father and his wife just kept the food coming. They overheard wonderful stories of classes, places, and new experiences. It was a coming together of a group of young people who were now forming new lives but still wanted to stay connected to old friends. Later, one of the teens said to this father, "Thinking about this get-together kept me going during the last few weeks at school." As teens develop new parts of themselves, they need touchstones to remind them of who they are and have been. Perhaps no one needs them more than those fresh out of high school.

Parents who have adjusted to a quieter, calmer home will at first be thrilled with their teen's arrival. But a 3:00 a.m. return home can bring back memories of all the day-to-day worries you have been happily released from. Push, pull. In and out. They want and need you, then they want and need to be independent.

Following this first big break, teens return to the intense flurry of papers and exams. This is usually a time of late nights with little room to breathe. By the time they come home for the winter holidays they have been through the wringer. Expect your teen to come home in desperate need of sleep, at least the first day or two.

During the first year, these holidays and the occasional visit from parents can help bridge the periods of hard work and soul-searching. If it is possible to visit your child at school, this is a great way to meet some of his new friends and peek inside his new life. Parent Weekend is a formal way for this to happen. If your child wants you to come and you can, this is an excellent way to connect—on his turf.

Other weekends may work well for visits, too. Our daughter sometimes stayed with us in the hotel when we came for a visit, and sometimes returned to her room for the night. We usually took her out to dinner with a friend or two, and for breakfast visited her favorite café. She enjoyed having a meal that she didn't have to budget for, and for me getting to know her friends was a treat. Sometimes we brought along our younger son, too. The two of them really missed each other, and these trips were particularly good for providing them some quality time together.

So much about this new adjustment relates to acknowledging the gigantic shift in the parent/teen relationship. Staying in touch is essential; it helps both parties move through the transition in a healthy, caring way. These teens are on their way, navigating their own lives. They need us less as guardians who tell them what to do, and more as guides who can point out the directions that are open to them and provide support along the way.

KEEPING AN EVEN KEEL AS TEENS COME AND GO

➢ Work on being the even keel for your teen. Be supportive and positive, even when your teen is struggling. This also entails taking care of yourself.

➢ Know that your teen is going to have hard moments, and gently remind her that this is part of the process—for everyone.

➤ Be interested in his classes and friends. This is the fun part, where it's easy to be encouraging.

➤ Encourage your teen to take charge of her life. Encourage her to talk to her roommate, resident adviser, professors, and work supervisors, to ask questions and get involved. Remember—encourage, but don't do it for her.

➤ Don't worship at the shrine of the empty room too much, but do allow the waves of missing him to move through you.

➤ Do what you can to keep the e-mail or phone contact going; let her needs lead the way.

➤ Use your intuition about when to visit and have other get-togethers. Again, factor in your student's needs. Planned gatherings can give both of you something to look forward to.

➤ Enjoy your teen's visits home, but don't be surprised by restlessness on his part.

➤ Every once in a while, remember something about your child that used to drive you crazy (the toilet seat, the dirty socks, etc.) and celebrate your liberation.

➤ Allow an awareness of new openings in your life to emerge as much as or even more than your sense of loss.

➤ Send notes or care packages. Students love to receive them, and it's a great way to remind your son or daughter that he or she is loved.

CHAPTER 12

Supporting Your Teen's Problem-Solving Skills

It's a tough age to parent—from 18 to the early 20s. They think they know everything, and you have so little control.

ALICE HOOLIHAN, MOTHER OF EIGHT, GRANDMOTHER, AND GREAT-GRANDMOTHER

There is no way around the fact that this time in teens' lives is about becoming more whole by taking risks, making mistakes, falling down and (hopefully) picking themselves up again, and expanding the boundaries of who they are and who they might become. It's exciting, and the effort is all theirs.

It can also be a lonely time; and it's always ironic to be lonely in the midst of so many people. Confusion and self-doubt are a part of the journey. Parents can expect that a teen may experiment or struggle at some point in a way that might be cause for concern: teens may not eat enough, or eat too much; party too much or close themselves up in their room; get sick (often from sleep deprivation); or not do well academically. When these situations arise, remember the following ideas:

- Offer support—When they need to talk, listen.
- Be discerning—Ask yourself: Is my child

struggling in a way that shows he needs my help or the help of a professional?

- Encourage—Let your teen know again and again that you are positive she can handle it.
- Let go—This is *the* ongoing challenge of parenting.

It is also helpful to notice and encourage the activities and friendships that help teens clarify who they are and bring out the best in them. Growing self-awareness and self-knowledge come in many forms and they deserve to be recognized and encouraged by us.

Providing Encouragement

According to one college student, "*No one* likes the first semester of college." While this statement is probably a gross exaggeration, it does speak to the fact that the first year away is a big adjustment, with so much adapting to do. It can be a lot of fun, but the fun doesn't come automatically. And often, parents hear only about the hard parts. It's so important not to overreact, but instead to listen and give a helpful suggestion *if your teen asks for it*. Don't hang on to your teen's issues—his moods and experiences can shift quickly.

Many parents do struggle with how to respond to despondent phone calls. One of the most important thing kids need at this age is for you to listen and support them. If your teen asks for your advice, seek understanding by asking more questions rather than offering solutions straight out. Ideally, she will talk herself into a solution. Help her figure out the pros and cons of an issue in order to make good choices. Many times, students just need to calm down. They also need to hear you say that you believe they *can* figure things out.

You can provide significant support just by being on the other end of the phone. It's not unusual to fret and worry over these calls, only to call back later and discover your child has moved on and now is in an entirely different and better place. So try not to let his down day cloud yours. It's entirely possible that, feeling better after talking to you, your son will walk across campus, run into a friend, make plans to meet later, and suddenly realize the test he was worried about or his irritation with his roommate seems manageable again.

Sometimes the call comes for advice about classes or choosing a major. If you can ask gently probing questions without providing the solution, you allow your child to recognize his own wisdom and give him the power to make decisions that will be his alone. Encouraging your child to list the pros and cons of various subjects or careers can help him clarify his choices. The challenge for parents is to respect his individuality. We do teens a disservice by thinking we know what is best for them. We can be sounding boards and we can point out factors they need to consider, but ultimately they must begin making their own choices. Our restraint—especially in the advice and answer-giving departments—is usually in a teen's best interest.

Holding Steady When a Teen Struggles

Anna kept getting phone calls several times a day from her daughter after she left for college. She was sad; she was unhappy; she wanted to come home every weekend. Hearing this is very difficult for a mother. Flooded with doubts about her own mothering, Anna floundered. Should she let her daughter come home every weekend? Should she make her tough it out? Why was it so hard for her—had she sheltered her daughter too much? Anna and Greg still had one son at home, but Anna was so worried about her daughter that she found herself distracted or snapping easily around the house.

Anna finally convinced her daughter to see a counselor on campus and agreed to let her come home every other weekend. Sometimes during the off weekend, Anna would go for a visit. Months went by. Then, early in the spring semester, Anna received a phone call and heard a lilt in her daughter's voice that she hadn't heard in a while. "Mom," she said, "my professor asked me to help organize a fund-raiser/ poetry reading!"

It wasn't the miracle cure, but it was the beginning of her daughter's finding her place in college. While she was working on the project, she made a new friend and the professor took a special interest in her, which made college feel like a warmer place. She also began exercising regularly and came away from her yoga class with another new friend.

When Your Child Wants to Drop Out

Sometimes a child leaves home when he isn't emotionally ready for the move. This happened to one couple whose son struggled with anxiety during his senior year of high school. Medication seemed to help immensely. But by the end of the summer between senior year and college, he was having more anxiety episodes. The parents tried their best to help him through. After they delivered him to school, his parents returned home to the empty nest they had been looking forward to, and found it to be—well, empty.

Almost right away, they began receiving phone calls from their son. The school didn't feel right, he didn't like his classes, he didn't get along with his roommate. He felt uncomfortable in his dorm room and in most of his classes. The parents were supportive over the phone and did everything they could to talk him into staying through the first semester, if not for the first year.

But he was just too miserable. After three weeks, he was

back home. So began a very difficult time. All of his friends were gone or busy with their own plans. He had to start from scratch to create a new plan. And the empty nest was suddenly no longer empty. This family's emotional adjustment made a 180-degree turn. Along with that shift, they worried and wanted to help their son, yet hold him accountable for his personal growth at the same time. It was not an easy path to navigate.

And so, they hobbled through the year. Made it clear he needed to earn some money and steadily work toward a plan for the following fall. They helped financially with a trip he wanted to take, mostly because they wanted him to feel like he had accomplished something for the year. And today his journey continues—a little traveling, working, and mapping out plans for the next year.

Sometimes a teen arrives at the school he has chosen and finds that even after weeks or months it does not feel like a good fit. There's no way to discern this clearly in advance, and especially early on. Most parents, when they are faced with this situation, will do everything they can to encourage their child to finish out the year and then reassess options. Is it the geographic space that is not working? Is there something internal that needs healing?

This experience is hard on parents. You can ask the questions and encourage your teen to stay long enough to find out what is really going on. You can use whatever financial help you are providing as leverage with your teen. But beyond those strategies, you're faced with a "letting go" process, which is always more difficult than it sounds.

When Your Teen Needs Professional Help

Sometimes teens do need more hands-on involvement from parents and health professionals. Discerning when your child may have a more serious problem can be a complicated task. But this is the first job for the parent of a troubled child, and it can take some time. Depression, eating disorders, alcohol abuse, and drug use signal real problems, and are often exacerbated by the challenges of living in a completely new environment. Yet, even if what you're hearing about in phone calls or e-mails is a more serious, long-lasting problem, it's wise to start by listening and asking questions to seek clarification. Panic or judgment on your part is (almost) never useful.

The need to take action or become more involved is clear if your child is asking for your help and input. Dropping out of school or earning unacceptable grades can create a situation in which it's clearly time for you to step in. Depression, substance addiction, gambling addiction, eating disorders, and other difficult illnesses clearly require professional intervention, as they can be lifelong or life-threatening if they are not dealt with promptly. Stepping in may mean calling the resident adviser or residential dean, or helping your student research available counseling and medical support systems. Counseling centers provide support groups that focus on specific problems. A psychologist can discern when a teen needs to sort through complex feelings and when she needs more formal intervention. If you know or sense that your teen is struggling, counseling is a good direction to point her in. If your teen is close enough to come home periodically and you have access to a good local professional, this can also be an option.

Part of a teen's path toward independence consists of finding ways to motivate himself. Anything you can do to encourage him to make his own discoveries is best in the long run. One mother told her son that she could not be the only person he talked to when he was going through a rough period. They were separated by half the country, and his angst over the phone was setting off her anxiety and helping him only minimally. A couple of weeks later he told his mom that he had found two resources: a counselor to talk to and an intramural team to join, which helped him feel more involved and less self-pitying. This took the heat off his mother. She was happy to be a sounding board, but it was also important to let her son know he needed to find other outlets on campus. She clearly communicated to him that it wasn't going to do him much good if she was his only support. So she gave him a push in the right direction, and he took it.

When Your Teen Is Depressed

Many (or most) teens will enjoy their classes and other activities, gradually settle in to new living arrangements, and start to make new friends. Sometimes, though, a teen will call, miserable—not just once in a while, but all the time. This happened to Beth and Jim. Their daughter had chosen a college only a few hours' drive away. She struggled throughout her freshman year. This was hard on Beth, who winced every time the phone rang. She took long walks, prayed, and visited her daughter often. Just as often, her daughter came home to visit.

Beth recommended that her teen see a professional counselor. After a period of time, the counselor suggested the young woman try an antidepressant for her depression. This period was difficult for Beth and Jim, neither of whom had ever struggled with depression, but they knew that if medication could help their daughter, then it would be worthwhile. Above all, they encouraged her to stick with school and make it through the year.

By the end of freshman year, their daughter was beginning to feel better. And by her junior year—still at the same school—she was active, involved, and happy. Looking back,

Beth and Jim can see that their daughter's depression probably began in high school. As a senior, this sensitive young woman had expressed hesitation and fear about her future. She was especially close to her parents and had avoided looking at colleges until the last minute, not really wanting to leave home.

While she needed a great deal of support to get through that first year, this teen's situation improved dramatically, and antidepressants were part of the solution. Beth and Jim had to let go of their preconceived notions about the meaning of antidepressants. They supported their daughter, learning on a daily basis to let go of control over the outcome. Tugs on the maternal heartstrings were powerful that freshman year, and Beth needed every ounce of her own support system to keep the depression from bringing her down. In their book *Letting Go: A Parents' Guide to Understanding the College Years,* Karen Levin Coburn and Madge Lawrence Treeger wisely suggest that newly launched young adults need "a listening ear that doesn't judge, even if we disagree, a sense of confidence that doesn't crumble when they do, and an adult anchor who provides perspective on the predictable but often painful changes that they are bound to go through."

One Teen's Struggle with Alcohol

Michelle's daughter, Lynn, had had one bad experience with alcohol in high school. Because of a family history of alcohol addiction, Michelle and her husband had had long talks with Lynn about this issue. While she was concerned about this part of her daughter's life, Michelle also greatly admired her daughter's strengths, talents, and hard work. Lynn's first two years of college went reasonably well. Things changed, however, in her junior year. She experienced a difficult breakup and indecision over her major. When Lynn came home between semesters for her holiday break, Michelle was upset to hear that her daughter's drinking had become a problem and was starting to interfere with Lynn's energy and happiness.

At the strong suggestion of both a campus counselor and another one at home, Lynn decided to take three months off from drinking. This proved difficult, and she often needed her mother's support over the phone. Lynn also joined a campus support group. The three months of abstention showed Lynn how extreme her usage had become. At the end of this dry period, Lynn felt ready to try moderate drinking. Michelle had mixed feelings, but was able to say, "I think it would be good for you to get ideas about this issue from your support group." Fortunately, Michelle was not her daughter's sole source of support and could share the role with her daughter's treatment group and counselors. Michelle also called on friends and sought out an Al Anon group that encouraged her as she supported her daughter's recovery. This helped Michelle draw a reasonable boundary between her life and her daughter's.

Encourage Self-Knowledge and Offer Hope

Conversations with many parents and school and health professionals confirm that when teens are in great need, parents can help tremendously by encouraging their self-awareness and self-knowledge. When your teen makes a mistake, let her talk about it; ask her to imagine what she could do differently next time. If her behavior needs changing, urge her to seek help and to consider how the behavior reflects or interferes with her goals. If she becomes physically ill, urge her to take responsibility for seeing a medical professional.

Encourage your teen to focus on positive activities—sports, journal-writing, workouts, dance, yoga, long walks, meditation, consulting a counselor, joining a support group—that provide relief (even temporary) from complex issues. Early adulthood is a time when teens acquire self-knowledge in an intense way. Not only is your teen learning to make choices on every front and monitor his own needs, but he is also experimenting, making mistakes, learning, healing, and facing the consequences of his actions. Offer him hope by reminding him of long-term goals, plans, and desires. Keep encouraging him to make choices that clarify who he is and where he wants to go.

Let Go

You may be familiar with the term "helicopter parents," those parents who hover in the background, ever ready to fix their children's problems for them. Some go so far as to call professors or college administrators to manage their teen's class, roommate, and sports issues. New parent terms keep emerging: the "lawn mower parent" who arrives *ahead* of the child to smooth the transition, mowing down any potential obstacles in the way; and the "stealth bomber" who swoops in out of nowhere and takes a chunk of skin off anybody with whom his or her child has been struggling.

A word to the wise: Constructive parenting is *always* about helping your child become his own person. Every person must learn how to deal with obstacles and conflict. As parents, we need to give our children the space to face and take care of their own problems. At times it will make sense to step in, but only after your teen has tried to handle the issue independently. And most of the time, teens *can* take care of it on their own. In the process, they learn that they can talk to professors and get good results, or speak to a resident adviser and make a new friend, or hash it out with their roommate and improve the living situation.

Sometimes it's harder to stand back than to dig in and take care of the problem ourselves. But as our kids head out into the world, they deserve the chance to fend for themselves. We can support them in the process by allowing them to take steps to stand up for themselves. Ultimately, it is far more rewarding for parent and child if your teen carves out her own solutions.

QUESTIONS TO ASK WHEN YOUR TEEN STRUGGLES

Remember to pause and breathe deeply before reacting to an important issue your teen brings up. Consider the following questions when a teen struggles:

- Do I listen to my teen when he asks for my attention?

- Am I supporting my teen in doing what she needs to do to deal with the problem?

- Do I ask questions that help my teen analyze the pros and cons?

- Am I able to discern when I need to step in and when I need to let go?

- Do I support my child by encouraging her to maintain healthy friendships and activities?

- Do I gently remind my teen to keep in mind the big picture—the goals that are important to him?

- Am I aware of resources available to my teen that will help him or her make changes?

- Do I encourage my child to use the resources?

➤ Do I actively encourage her to take steps toward gaining self-awareness?

➤ Do I remember to ask what makes him happy or challenged in the course of a day—which classes, friends, and activities bring meaning to his life?

➤ Have I been paying attention to my own needs?

➤ Do I have my own formal or informal support group to help get me through the "letting go" transition?

CHAPTER 13

Your Teen and You: The Emerging Adult-to-Adult Relationship

As our children work their way into adulthood, we get to enjoy (as well as worry about) who they are and who they are becoming. Because we have lived together for so many years, we are bound to have activities to share, topics of conversation to keep us chatting, and shared memories, both bad and good, to chew over. As imperfect as it can feel at times, the bond between parent and child is ongoing and powerful.

The Power of Your Voice

Anna Quindlen writes in her collection of essays *Loud and Clear* about her connection to her college-age son at a most poignant moment in shared history—the morning of 9/11: "One of the mementos I have kept from that morning are three identical e-mails from our son at college who could not get through (by phone) on his birthday (9/11) or three days afterward. Each one is dated September 11, 2001, and says in capital letters: I REALLY NEED TO HEAR YOUR VOICE."

Simply and powerfully, Quindlen describes the elemental connection we hope to, and in most cases do, have with our emerging adult children. What her son wanted in that shared moment of trauma wasn't answers, and he knew he couldn't come home; he simply and powerfully wanted to connect. Voices tether us in this physical world.

Cell phones and e-mail have profoundly changed the landscape of this emerging relationship. It is far easier now than ever before for parents to stay in touch and get a sense of how a teen's classes, activities, work situation, and relationships are being handled. Ideally, this makes for stronger friendships between parent and child. And although the power balance between parent and child tends to be based on old patterns, this changes as the child grows. The first years out of high school, however, are definitely a time of shifting back and forth between the old, comfortable ways and the newer, more fluid ways of relating.

A Personal Story

I got along well enough with my daughter when she was in high school, but by no means were we an intimately close mother-daughter pair. So when the calls from college became more frequent, and she asked to do things together with me while she was home on break (things I had always invited her to do with me before without much success, such as running and going out for coffee), it was a pleasure. She wanted my opinion in a way she had never been open to before. Of course, the old ways occasionally erupted, but we made new strides in our relationship.

Around the holidays, I've noticed a familiar pattern in my circle of friends. How excited we all become about our kids' homecomings! How we all anticipate seeing them and being with them, so grown up and pleasant. And then, as the break draws to a close, a mixture of sadness and relief always settles in. We admit it would be nice not to have to share the car anymore. Getting back to normal hours will feel good; and no more dirty towels on the floor that we had to keep reminding them about. And the way they wanted to stay out so late? That, too, was only momentary.

Nevertheless, having my daughter show an interest in activities we can do together has been a pleasure. The summer between her freshman and sophomore years we took a canoe trip, just the two of us. Even the fact that she would agree to a trip like this, carving time out of her summer to be with just me, was a huge shift and a sign of her emerging adult self. For five days, we canoed, camped, swam, and fished. We shared our love for hot coffee at sunrise. We laughed—loudly and freely—the day we caught fish after fish. I baited hooks; she reeled in a ton of fish, and I caught a few myself. Later, I cleaned them.

Sometimes my daughter could read the map better than I, or was more likely to make a clear decision about the next direction to take. At other times, I took the lead. We traded roles—which is how friendships work. This is not to say that there weren't moments of frustration or irritation with one another. There were. But for the most part, the two of us were on equal ground, getting along, enjoying the scenery, enjoying the action, and enjoying each other. But if you had told me a year earlier that I would have such an experience with my daughter, I would not have believed you.

As parents, if we are lucky we will be able to enjoy the capable young adult coming to the surface, the one we have helped guide and foster. As my own daughter grows into her interests, I am happy to see that she can be independent, yet also strongly bonded to me and to her family.

Sharing Interests and Activities

Jerry spoke of how his son Sam took up cross-country skiing in high school. His action revived an old passion of Jerry's in the same sport. Throughout high school, the two of them skied often together, and Jerry attended all of the races. The sport continued to be a bond for them after Jerry's son left for college. They looked forward to skiing together whenever Sam was home on a holiday break, and they made a deal to take part in one long race together during the winter season. The two shared skiing tips through e-mails, and they traded details of their workout schedules. At times when Jerry worried about his son during bouts of homesickness, conversations about the next ski race or workout helped smooth the path.

Many families share a love of music. The parents in one family described how they periodically meet one or more of their children in various cities to attend concerts together. The anticipation of the event works as a treat that can help any of them get through a tough day. This planned gathering also serves as a reward for hard work in the meantime. Long periods of separation sometimes exist between these events, but they provide a much-needed point of family connection.

Another family plans trips together with their late-teen and twentysomething children. School breaks provide a natural framework within which they can schedule plans. The parents' busy work schedules had made travel difficult when their children were younger, but now the family is able to plan, look forward to, and enjoy vacations together. These trips have been a way for the parents to continue being involved in their children's lives in a way that still acknowledges their independent paths. Together, they have hiked miles of trails. After years of hounding kids to practice musical instruments and do homework, it is a treat for the parents to explore the world with their adult children and enjoy the people they have become.

Of course, many of us don't have the kind of budget that supports extended trips for the holidays, but parents can still make a point of planning fun and relaxing things to do together at home. Take long walks or runs together, seek out all the best thrift stores in town for great deals, plan workouts together, or find a yoga class or bargain matinee. Rent old movies and curl up in your favorite room to watch them together at night. Many families enjoy cooking meals together and trying new recipes on each other. During the day, while parents are at work, teens often jump at the chance to have the house to themselves, reveling in the familiar. It can be a good break from all the frenzy and excitement of dorm life.

When I was in college, I came home on most school breaks. Sometimes I was able to pick up hours at my old job to earn extra money. But I also used the time at home as an informal retreat, doing at a slower pace all the things that I loved and missed—biking, skating, skiing, and hanging out with my family at the dinner table in the early evening. If friends were around, I'd meet them and go out at night. There was something very simple and comforting about just being home. It was a touchstone time for me and helped ground me. I was always ready to head back to a more exciting life, renewed and rested. This kind of experience remains valid and very much available to teens today.

It's often said that "once a parent, always a parent." I see the truth of the phrase in my parents' particular experience. Now in their 90s, they still look out for all eight of their (now middle-aged) children and probably in some way still have their worries about each one of us. But we no longer expect help from our parents in the same way that we did when we were much younger. So enjoying each other's company can be mutual. This is the ultimate goal of letting go. Ideally, as our children become more independent, more their own persons living their own lives, they and we will enjoy spending time together—in all the many ways we can.

NURTURING LIFELONG CONNECTIONS TO YOUR TEEN

➤ Establish a healthy way to communicate with your teen via cell phone, e-mail, instant messaging, letter writing, or whatever way works best for both of you.

➤ Be receptive to the times when your child just needs to hear your voice, and you just need to hear his.

➤ Use your shared interests with your teen as a way to connect. Plan to enter a race together, cook together, share a favorite book together, go bargain-hunting at thrift stores, or attend a concert or play together. Make plans in advance so that you can both anticipate and look forward to getting together.

➤ Make plans to be with your teen on school breaks, during visits, or at other special times. Organize a special meal or outing together.

➤ If you can, arrange a trip with your child, for the weekend or even longer. Ask for help with the planning.

CHAPTER 14

Honoring the Parental Passage

She's running ahead, pushing forward, leaning into it, not looking back. Me, I'm not ready. I'm not done . . . there is so much left to do . . . so much of the world we didn't see. We never lived abroad or learned a second language. We only wore one matching mother/daughter outfit. How can it be over? I'm not done yet.

DANA ESSEX, *"BUT I'M NOT READY YET"*

Maybe there comes a point in life where we are all faced with ourselves. Perhaps when a partner abruptly leaves us or when our children move on or when we are drawing our last breaths, but at some point . . . we are faced with our own reflection of who we truly are.

JULIANN HEATH, *"THE LETTING GO"*

The realization that 18 years had passed in the blur of parent-child fullness hit me hard. It's a moment worth pausing for and reflecting upon. Two decades sounds like such a long time, and in many ways it is, but as you send your child off—to college, work, travel, or service—the reality of the phrase "time flies" settles decisively in your consciousness. Inevitably, an awareness of your own aging is connected to this fact, poignantly and powerfully.

Remember the equally shocking, but infinitely promising, beginning of the parenting journey? In one swift moment the life before children is gone, and suddenly baby is here. Cries and needs take over—*really* take over. Not a minute of the day goes by unaffected by this immense change.

When you return from that first college drop-off and wander the house, the change feels equally sudden and seismic. There one day, gone the next, even though you knew it was inevitable. Even though there were moments you couldn't wait for it to come. "It" is this odd, peculiar, strange, expansive, and unnerving emptiness.

Fathers and mothers offered candid assessments of their own coming to terms with their children's departures:

"It felt lonely."

"I felt as if I'd been fired from a job I was so devoted to."

"I didn't find the adjustment so hard, maybe because my son chose a school only a couple of hours away. I loved not having to worry about his weekend hours anymore, and yet he came home often enough that I didn't get too lonely for him. For me, it was the best of both worlds."

"There was so much conflict between us senior year that my wife and I breathed a sigh of relief when our daughter left home. After a long break, our relationship with her began to slowly improve."

"I cried for four days after he left for college."

"After I dropped my daughter at the airport, I almost had to breathe into a paper bag. She was heading into such a huge change: how would she handle it? Then I realized I was heading into an equally huge change."

"The adjustment wasn't as hard as I thought it would be. I do notice that we are freer. Rather than having to adjust my day to my daughter's needs, schedules, or hungers, I can do my own thing. There's a lot about that I like. Of course, it helps that I'm going to visit her soon."

"At first I didn't think it was such a big deal. But then it started sinking in . . . at an almost instinctual level. I felt a deep loss, even as my remaining teen was driving me crazy."

"The shift was physically painful . . . I felt it in my chest."

Whether you've sent a child off in the last month, the last year, or even earlier, the emotional impact of the event has deep resonance. Feelings are still so close to the surface. How ready people were to talk about this shift, and how little opportunity or space for this kind of talk there is in our efficient culture. But there is nothing efficient or controllable about grieving. One has to walk through, talk through, and move through some of those feelings to finally see the empty space as an opportunity.

Identity Shift

This past summer, our youngest child took off from the dock in a small boat to visit his friend, who was a 10- or 15-minute boat ride away. It was the first time he had piloted the boat so far by himself. My husband and I helped him load the boat and launch it. We stood on the dock, watching him move out of sight.

Whatever he might run into—unexpected waves from a passing boat, motor trouble, not knowing the way as well as he thought he did—he would have to figure it out for himself. We had prepared him as best we could. He had taken smaller trips, and we had let him drive with one of us in the boat. Now it was up to him to drive safely, pay attention, deal with the unexpected, and find his way. And there I was, back on the dock. What chores, passions, desires, and needs was I going to move toward in the space opening up in front of me? For this was the beginning of his independence; that, I could see.

Whether parents are married or single, passionately involved in a career or other pursuit, what looms large is the necessary identity shift that occurs with our letting go of our children. How many times in times past did you introduce yourself as so-and-so's father or mother? When you send your first child out into the world, there are many echoes of loss. Perhaps above all is the alteration of your identity as a hands-on parent of that child.

Of course, you are still a parent, but your role has changed. The earlier days of active parenting are certainly busy and demanding. And during your child's senior year, your parenting obligations and time demands grow to almost epic proportions. The end is filled with a frenzy of last-minute preparations. And then, your teen is launched. You watch your teen go—with some fear and trepidation mingled with pride and excitement for your teen child—and know that this is the natural progression of life.

Knowing this, nevertheless I cannot shake an image of myself left on the dock. Left with my questions, and, of course, at its core, the *one:* "Now who am I? Now what am I going to do with my life?" The questions have many permutations—"What will make my life as meaningful as parenting was?" "What are my desires and goals now?" "Will he be okay?" Nor can I shake the image of my youngest child on the water, navigating his way alone. Whatever wind or waves or weather he faced, he would have to maneuver by himself. When I knew he had arrived safely, I breathed a sigh of relief—a wistful pride overtaking the beating heart of fear.

So. A teen is launched. And you who have helped her launch can take all the energy you put into the launching— hugely significant energy—and direct it in the ways you most want and need. What matters now? As the last one leaves home, it does become our job to sort through who we have been as parents and how we want to spend the next years of our lives. Weren't there days we longed for this kind of physical and emotional space?

I was aware of some regrets, of a sense of not having done enough or done it well enough. But I was also aware of the kind of dedication I had poured into parenting because the lack of a need for day-to-day hands-on parenting left a large vacancy in my sense of being. Although I still had one at home, the reality loomed that within a few years he too would be shoving off from shore.

Across the board, parents experience at least a momentary sense of emptiness when their child leaves home, regardless of other work and family commitments. At the core, most of us care so deeply about our children and put so much time, energy, and concern into their daily well-being that when they walk out the door into the next chapter of their lives, we feel a gaping hole. More than one mother I talked to said, "Now I must finally look at my relationships and work life. For the first time in a long time, I have the time and energy to spare, and believe me, they could both use some attention."

Gifts of the Empty Nest

Not all that comes with the empty nest is sadness. Parents interviewed for this book spoke of enjoying and appreciating the decrease in chaos that comes when children leave home. Gas tanks stay at their expected levels, keys can be found where you leave them, and piles of clothes or paperwork strewn across the house tend to disappear.

Many spoke of choosing meals that they and their partners were interested in sharing, choices not dependent upon kids' likes and dislikes. Many other choices no longer require prolonged negotiation. Life is simpler and quieter. More extroverted parents may miss the excitement of constant teen-inspired action, but many treasure the peacefulness. Across the board, parents seem to enjoy the decrease in clutter. One parent commented, "I don't think of myself as shallow, but every day I appreciate the fact that I can set something down and find it still in its place the next day, not covered up by other stuff." Another parent exclaimed, "We get to choose the movie *and* the restaurant now. So much less negotiating!"

One mother shared an additional insight. When her youngest was a college freshman, she began to set personal goals for herself. She trained for and ran a marathon. She took art classes and started painting again. She backed off from volunteer commitments she had made for years, although not giving them up completely, and gradually began to shift some focus back to herself. Through these actions, she created some momentum; she didn't have to start completely from scratch when it came to knowing who she was.

Gratitude and Reflection

As you move on to the next era in your life, it is helpful (and important) to cast a reflective eye on the time you've spent with your teen. Even if you have other children at home, take time to notice what you did for and with this child. If we all really allow ourselves to ponder this achievement, we might even be impressed. We might find enough harvest here to circumvent any regret.

Recently, I dug through old skating photos of my oldest child and found pictures of myself pulling her across the ice on a sled, holding her hand when she was first learning to skate. There were other photos, too—of her ice shows, of props we all scrounged to come up with. I remember the enjoyment of choosing the music and costumes, even if our input wasn't always taken. What was important was that we were involved in the discussion together.

The momentary pause with these photos in hand caused me to reflect on how much joy we had all shared in this part of our family life. I could remember, proudly, our daughter's dedication to her sport, which often entailed early-morning drives to practice. This was just one small aspect of her life, but I enjoyed thinking about the memories it sparked—our full parental support and our thrill in watching her out on the ice. And I still love to go skating with my daughter, even though she has long since surpassed my skating abilities.

Anna spoke of visiting her daughter in New York City and the way her daughter became her travel guide—showing her mother the subway ins and outs. Anna's daughter had taken advantage of many opportunities during her few months in the city. Anna tagged along one day to her daughter's internship in a theater studio. She could see that her daughter was a valued worker and had learned her way around the light board, sound board, and stage. She even sat in as accompanist on the piano once in a while, and had gotten to know many of the actors and musicians, too. Anna felt a real sense of personal accomplishment as she watched her daughter, and knew that she had raised a young woman who knew how to take care of herself, challenge herself, and rise to meet that challenge.

In terms of reflection, we all have regrets. It's only human. We become so tied to the things we didn't get around to doing or the things we did imperfectly. But it's crucial to take time to think about, write about, or talk about what was accomplished. Think of all your child's areas of interest. What activities or lessons did you support? How many homework projects did you help with? How many birthday cakes did you bake? What rituals did you create (even the simple and wacky ones)? How many favorite meals did you prepare? Marvel now at how your support contributed to your teen's talents, abilities, and capacity for thinking, caring, and reasoning as she or he now maneuvers through the world.

What Next?

The world opens up—for both of you—as your teen launches into a new life and you say good-bye to day-by-day parenting. It's a poignant time, yet it carries its own possibility for renewal. Those were sweet years—many or most, if not all. A healthy farewell to that era includes time for reflection and gratitude for all the wonderful gifts of those lived-in years and for the gift of parenting. It is a rich and deeply human experience. As you take out your lists of goals and dreams, let yourself be inspired in the same way that you have worked so hard to inspire your children: to be their best, to explore the world, to live fully, and to have some fun along the way.

TIME TO REFLECT AND LOOK FORWARD

➤ Acknowledge to yourself a job well done.

➤ Recognize any regrets you may have, but don't dwell on them. Know that no one "lets go" perfectly.

➤ Make a list of what you and your child did together that worked out well.

➤ Take time for gratitude—for your child's presence in your life, for the gifts he or she has brought to your family, and for all the supportive people who have helped you along the way.

➤ Thank people who have aided you and your child on this journey: other parents, teachers, coaches, faith leaders, neighbors, relatives, community members, and friends.

➤ Grieve when you need to—to acknowledge what is ending and what is just now beginning.

➤ Create and make use of your own support system.

➤ Get help when you feel yourself floundering—isn't that what you would advise your child to do?

➤ Explore the open spaces in your life, and consider that you have opportunities for new and meaningful experiences just as your teen does.

➤ Love and cherish the changing relationship that you and your teen are forging together.

➤ Post your own goals and dreams on the wall—this is your time, too.

Resources for
Parents and Teens

A HIGH SCHOOL TIME LINE
FOR PARENTS AND TEENS

Freshman Year

☐ Encourage your teen to work for good grades. No matter what she decides to do, good grades will be an asset.

☐ Be supportive of your child's involvement in extra-curricular activities—they give teens another avenue for building confidence and exploring interests and talents.

☐ Meet with your teen's school counselor and, if available, check out the college and career center. The more you know about available resources the more you can direct your teen toward them.

☐ Check out yourself and encourage your teen to know what high school courses are required for college or other career paths in which he might be interested.

☐ Help your teen become familiar with NCAA requirements if she thinks she wants to play sports in college.

☐ Help your teen keep an academic portfolio and record of extracurricular activities.

☐ Work together with your teen on ways to save money for college or trade school.

Sophomore Year

☐ If your child is college-bound, have her check with the school counselor in September about taking the PSAT (the SAT prep test) in October. Also have her ask about taking the PLAN test (the ACT prep test). Both are preliminary tests, but can be very helpful to take. Missed it this time around? They can also be taken junior year.

☐ Encourage your child to continue being a good student, and keep records of his grades and writing samples. Help your teen begin a student résumé.

☐ Support your child's involvement in extracurricular activities, and keep records of her participation.

☐ In April, if your teen is college-bound, remind him to register for two of the June SAT II subject tests.

Junior Year

☐ In September, remind your college-bound teen to register for the October Preliminary Scholastic Aptitude Test (PSAT). The junior year PSAT score can qualify a student for the National Merit scholarship competition and for National Achievement and National Hispanic Scholars Programs. Scores will not be used for college admissions.

☐ Encourage your teen to study and read—junior year grades are very important for college admissions and any other career path as well.

☐ In December, register for the February ACT if your student is planning to take it.

☐ Encourage your child to use her school counselor, teachers, and the college and career center to begin or continue researching her options.

☐ In February, suggest to your student that he meet with the school counselor and begin making a preliminary list of colleges or other paths that interest him.

- [ ] If a Career Day or College Fair Day is held at your teen's school or nearby, do everything you can to encourage your child to take advantage of this great opportunity for research.

- [ ] Spring and summer after the junior year can be a good time to plan a family trip that focuses on college visits.

- [ ] Look around at your resources and help connect your teen with a mentor or professional in the areas of her interests.

- [ ] Remind your student to begin requesting admissions forms and guidelines from colleges or other programs that interest him. Most can be requested online, and you can also call or write the program for materials or visit the career center at school.

Senior Year

- [ ] Go over with your teen all of the applications required for admission to college and review financial aid forms together.

- [ ] Be sure your teen meets with his counselor early in the year to plan steps for college, vocational or trade school, or other life plans.

- [ ] Remind your student to ask teachers and counselors for required letters of recommendation ahead of time, preferably three to six weeks early, and give them recommendation forms along with stamped, addressed envelopes.

☐ In September, remind your college-bound child to register for the October/November SAT or September/October ACT.

☐ Remind your student that the test backup plan is to register in October for the December/January SAT or December ACT.

☐ Help provide a filing system for your student. Encourage her to keep records of all test scores and copies of applications and financial aid forms.

☐ Be sure your child completes the Common Application (online at www.commonapp.org).

☐ Create, with your teen, a highly visible calendar for all application deadlines—and check it regularly!

☐ Create a checklist that stays available and visible to both you and your student.

☐ Remind your teen that December is Early Decision month for colleges. Late April is the Regular Decision time for most colleges. Be supportive and understanding of the pressure your child feels in these last weeks.

☐ Understand the courage it takes a teen to try a different path if he or she chooses not to go to college. Congratulate him or her on having a plan.

☐ In May and June, encourage your child to study, sleep, and do well on final tests and grades. Enjoy the last special events with friends and family.

☐ June—graduation! Celebrate your huge accomplishment—both parents and teen.

THE COLLEGE APPLICATION PACKAGE

Your teen's final application for each school should include the following elements:

- ☐ Common Application (send by mail or online at www.commonapp.org)
- ☐ Supplemental school applications (if applicable; send by mail or online)
- ☐ Application fee (send by mail or online with a credit card, or send a fee waiver form, if it applies to your family's financial situation)
- ☐ Audition tape, arts portfolio, or scientific research summary (send if applicable)
- ☐ Confidential recommendations sent by teachers and school counselor
- ☐ Transcripts and school reports sent by the school counselor
- ☐ Test results (request the testing administration to send these)
- ☐ Optional: student résumé

KEY DATES FOR THE HIGH SCHOOL SENIOR YEAR CALENDAR

Be sure to mark each of these dates clearly on your family calendar:

- ☐ Final school project deadlines
- ☐ Application deadlines (college, vocational school, public service, or work plans)
- ☐ FAFSA financial aid deadline (see Chapter 6, Navigating the Financial Aid Maze)
- ☐ Test dates for college entrance exams
- ☐ Special senior events—academic, sports, arts, and others
- ☐ College visits (campus tours, admissions office interviews, auditions, family trips)
- ☐ Alumni interviews (if applicable)
- ☐ Auditions or tryouts (if applicable)

Bibliography

Benson, Peter. *Sparks: How Parents Can Help Ignite the Hidden Strengths of Teenagers.* San Francisco: Jossey-Bass, 2008.

> Helps parents identify and support their teen's motivating passions in life.

Bolles, Richard Nelson, Carol Christen, and Jean M. Blomquist. *What Color Is Your Parachute? For Teens: Discovering Yourself, Defining Your Future.* Berkeley, CA: Ten Speed Press, 2006.

> A thoughtful, step-by-step guide to vocational and career identification and values clarification for teens.

Coburn, Karen Levin, and Madge Lawrence Treeger. *Letting Go: A Parents' Guide to Understanding the College Years* (4th ed.). New York: HarperCollins, 2003.

> Offers support to parents as they guide teens into and through the college years.

Cohen, Harlan. *The Naked Roommate: And 107 Other Issues You Might Run Into in College.* Naperville, IL: Sourcebooks, Inc., 2009.

> Provides a wise, close-up look at today's college campus.

The College Board, *The College Board Book of Majors.* New York: The College Board, 2008.
> Updated annually. Summarizes academic majors and what they entail.

Covey, Sean. *The 7 Habits of Highly Effective Teens.* New York: Franklin Covey Fireside, 1998.
> Offers teens a clear guide to identifying goals and naming steps to reach them.

Ehrenhaft, George. *Writing a Successful College Application Essay: The Key to College Admission.* Hauppauge, NY: Barron's Educational Series, 1993.
> Step-by-step advice on writing an application essay that reveals a student's voice, personality, and interests. Covers topic choice, writing the first draft, polishing, and editing the final essay.

Essex, Dana. "But I'm Not Ready Yet." Minneapolis: Unpublished essay, 2008.

Fiske, Edward B. *Fiske Guide to Colleges.* Naperville, IL: Sourcebooks, Inc., 2009.
> Updated annually. Lists public and private colleges in every state and provides summaries of academic strengths, sports programs, financial aid statistics, tuition costs, test score averages, and more.

Fiske, Edward B., and Bruce G. Hammond. *Fiske Real College Essays That Work.* Naperville, IL: Sourcebooks, Inc., 2009.
> Includes 100+ college essay examples and points out what makes them work.

Heath, Juliann. "The Letting Go." Minneapolis: Unpublished essay, 2008.

Loveland, Elaina. *Creative Colleges: A Guide for Student Actors, Artists, Dancers, Musicians and Writers.* Belmont, CA: SuperCollege, LLC, 2008.
 Offers tips for auditioning and assembling arts portfolios. Includes sample résumés, essays, and information from admission officers and admitted students.

Ostrum, Eva. *The Thinking Parent's Guide to College Admissions: The Step-by-Step Program to Get Kids into the Schools of Their Dreams.* New York: Penguin Books, 2006.
 A detailed look at every aspect of the college admissions process.

Pope, Loren. *Colleges That Change Lives: 40 Schools That Will Change the Way You Think about Colleges.* New York: Penguin Books, 2006.
 Describes small liberal arts colleges focused on academic potential, personal values, initiative, and leadership abilities. Includes anecdotes from students, professors, and graduates.

Seghers, Linda, ed. *Peterson's Colleges for Students with Learning Disabilities or ADD* (8th ed.). Lawrenceville, NJ: Peterson's, 2006.
 Profiles 900+ two- and four-year colleges with structured/proactive collegiate programs, as well as those with self-directed/decentralized programs for the student with learning disabilities. Includes legal considerations and documentation required for college eligibility.

The Princeton Review. *College Essays That Made a Difference* (3rd ed.). Princeton, NJ: The Princeton Review, 2008.
> Includes real essays of students who applied to and were accepted by highly selective colleges and universities, along with complete application profiles of students and information about why they were accepted or rejected by schools.

Quindlen, Anna. *Loud and Clear*. New York: Ballantine Books, 2005.
> Poignant and to-the-point essays on family life and myriad other topics.

Solorzano, Lucia. *Barron's Best Buys in College Education*. Hauppauge, NY: Barron's Educational Series, 2008.
> Gives detailed information about affordable schools under $20,000 a year and describes their academic programs, campus environments, and unique features. Includes single-sex schools.

Steinberg, Jacques. *The Gatekeepers: Inside the Admissions Process of a Premier College*. New York: Viking, 2002.
> Follows real students and college admissions counselors over the course of a year and describes the application cycle in detail.

Stewart, Mark Alan, and Cynthia C. Muchnick. *Best College Admission Essays*. Lawrenceville, NJ: Peterson's, 2004.
> Includes 50 sample college application essays with tips on writing style, essay themes, content selection. Advice from college admission officers as well.

U.S. Department of Labor. *Occupational Outlook Handbook 2009: An Up-to-Date Guide to Today's Job Market.* New York: Skyhorse Publishing, 2008.
Updated biannually.

Wilson, Erlene B. *100 Best Colleges for African American Students.* New York: Penguin Books, 1998.
Summarizes admissions requirements of colleges selected by the author for their campus atmosphere, quality of race relations, supportive programming, social organizations, cultural and career opportunities, and prominent graduates.

Acknowledgments

I would first like to thank Search Institute for having faith in this project from the very beginning. A special debt of gratitude goes to my editor, Susan Wootten, and her team of readers for invaluable help honing, fine-tuning, shaping, and polishing this book. Many thanks also to Kate Brielmaier for guiding this book through the final stages.

A special thanks to all education professionals who work with teens, especially those who took time out of their busy schedules to share their experiences with me: Mary Morseth, Connie Overhue, Danielle Jastrow, and Adrienne Diercks. Their insights nourished many pages in this book.

So many parents and teens contributed their stories, experiences, and insights to this book. Some did so casually, almost unwittingly; others spent time deliberately sharing their experiences in great depth. I thank all of you, both named and unnamed. Your experiences are the heart and soul of this book, and I couldn't have done it without your generosity. Deep thanks to Celia Davis, Brigid O'Hara Chase, Laurel, Karen Ballor, Darlene Havers, John Curtiss, Kay Costello, Marti Hickner, John Floberg, Giovanni M., Eric S., William D., Christine McVay, Susan White, Darcy Berglund, Laura and Bill Hoolihan, and Chris Fisher.

Thank you to Juliann Heath and Dana Essex, who shared their wonderful writings on this topic with me and allowed me to quote some of their work in these pages. Excerpts by Juliann Heath are from her essay "The Letting Go."

Excerpts from Dana Essex are from her essay "But I'm Not Ready Yet."

A special thanks to the authors and publishers of two books I found to be especially helpful: *The Naked Roommate: And 107 Other Issues You Might Run Into in College,* by Harlan Cohen, and *Letting Go: A Parents' Guide to Understanding the College Years,* by Karen Levin Coburn and Madge Lawrence Treeger.

To my running and coffee group, whose hard-earned wisdom spills over the edge of the cup and ends up in my writing—thank you, thank you, thank you to Beth Dooley, Leslie Bush, Mary Reyelts, Randy Lebedoff, and Angie Lillehei.

To the many people with whom I had fleeting encounters—offering me insights and wisdom, and repeated affirmations of the huge sweep of this transition for parents—I am grateful to all of you.

Index

529 savings plans, 86, 87

academic transcript, 62
acceptance, to college, 71, 72
activities, sharing, 159–162
admissions process, 72
Advanced Placement classes, 105
alcohol, 108, 109, 114, 126, 150
  struggling with, 152, 153
American College Test (ACT), 57, 70
AmeriCorps, 34–37, 46
application deadlines, 70
auditions, 65, 66, 94

budgeting, 76, 78, 82
  tools, online, 79

care packages, 143
career
  centers, 46, 58
  inventories, 60, 72
certificates of deposit, 87
change of schools, 24
checking account, 77
Chura, Hillary, 88, 91
Coburn, Karen Levin, 79, 152
Cohen, Harlan, 109, 126, 128

College Board Book of Majors, The, 11
College Level Examination Program (CLEP), 105
college
  application process, 47, 48
  guidebooks to, 50
  researching, 47–49
  visits, 64, 65, 72
Colleges That Change Lives, 51, 52
communication, 113, 118, 127, 139, 140, 143, 162
community service programs, 34
counseling centers, 41
course catalog, 106
course registration, 113
Coverdell Education Savings Account (ESA), 87, 88
Creative Colleges, 51
credit, 78
  cards, 79, 80, 82
  history, 81
  reports, 79, 81, 82
  scores, 79, 82

deadlines, 53, 54, 113
decisions, 24, 67, 68

Department of Education, 91
departure, 27, 28
depression, 150–152
Diercks, Adrienne, 6, 7
Dillon, Sam, 70
disappointment, 13, 14, 16
drop off, 130, 131
dropping out, 148–150
due dates, 113

early action, 69–71
early decisions, 69–71
eating disorders, 150
education deductions, 98
education tax credits, 98
empty nest 168
essay, 63, 69
Essex, Dana, 139
Expected Family Contribution (EFC), 91, 92
expenses, sharing, 102, 104
experiential programs, 12

FAFSA, 89–92, 99
Fair Isaac, 82
Federal Pell Grant, 95
Federal Perkins Loan Program, 95
Federal Supplemental Educational Opportunity Grant (FSEOG), 95
Financial aid, 72, 83
financing higher education, 84, 85
Fiske Guide to Colleges, 11, 50

freshman orientation, 104–106
friendships, 111, 126, 127,128

Gates Millennium Scholars Program, 93
Glasser, William, 55
goals, 7–9, 13, 14, 16, 41, 52, 53, 119, 155, 168
good-byes, 21, 22, 131, 132, 134, 135
grades, 150
graduation day, 29
grants, 92, 93
gratitude, 169–171
grieving, 20, 171

health care, 104, 125
Heath, Julian, 22
Holland, John, 10, 61
home, living at, 115
Hope Credit, 87, 98

identity shift, 165–167
illness, family, 15
independent living, 101, 121
interest inventories, 10
interests, 10, 159–162
Internal Revenue Service, 86, 98
International Baccalaureate (IB) programs, 105

Job Corps, 34
jobs, full-time, 33
journal, 21

Kuder Career Planning
    System, 61

leaders, 15
learning disability, 116, 117
letter of recommendation, 63
letting go, 154, 155, 156
*Letting Go: A Parents' Guide to
    Understanding the College
    Years*, 79, 152
Lewin, Tamar, 89
Lifetime Learning Credit, 88,
    98
Lions Clubs, 92
living alone, 121, 122
Loud and Clear, 157

managing time, 106, 107
mementos, home, 102
mentor, 7–10
military, enlisting in, 43–45
Muchnick, Jeanne, 33
Myers-Briggs Type Indicator,
    10

*Naked Roommate: And 107
    Other Issues You Might Run
    Into In College, The*, 109,
    127, 128
National Endowment for
    Financial Education
    (NEFE), 76, 80, 82
National Outdoor Leadership
    School (NOLS), 38, 46
NCAA Initial-Eligibility
    Clearinghouse Form, 93

*Occupational Outlook
    Handbook*, 11
*Occupational Outlook
    Quarterly*, 11

packing, 102, 113, 129, 130,
    134
Parent Loans for
    Undergraduate Students
    (PLUS), 96, 97
parent loans, 96
parental passage, 163–165
parenting
    shift, 137, 138
    style, 107
Parenting Teens Online, 33
Police Explorers, 42
portfolios, 65, 66, 94
professional help, teen needs,
    149, 150
public service, 42

Quindlen, Anna, 157

regular admission deadlines,
    69
rejection, 72
relationships, 110–112
    long-distance, 112
    with teachers, 54
research, 72, 118
rolling admission, 69
roommates, 102, 103, 119, 124,
    127, 128
    freshmen, 122
Rotary Clubs, 92

rules
    family, 113
    reinventing, 107, 108

safety awareness, 125, 126, 128
savings bonds, 87
scholarships, 92, 93, 98
    arts, 94, 95
    athletic, 93, 94
Scholastic Aptitude Test
    (SAT), 57, 70
school counselor, 54–57, 62,
    105
school, applying for, 61, 62
self-assessment, 10
Self-Directed Search, 10, 61
senior events, 27, 29
senior year, difficulties, 23
sexual behavior, 109, 110, 114
skilled trades, 41, 42
sleep, 128
    deprivation, 124
Strong Interest Inventory, 60

Student Aid Report (SAR), 91
student loans, 95, 96, 99
SUCCESS, 6, 12
support, 18, 19, 44, 152, 155

tax breaks, 100
teacher recommendation, 64
traveling, 13, 38–40
Treeger, Madge Lawrence, 79,
    152
tuition expense, 83

UTMA/UGMA accounts, 88

visits
    college and career center,
        58, 59
    from teen, 140–142
    home, 143
vocational schools, 33

waiting, 67, 68
work-study jobs, 97, 98